Motivating
Students and Teachers
in an Era of Standards

Richard Sagor

Association for Supervision and Curriculum Development
Alexandria, VA USA

®

Association for Supervision and Curriculum Development
1703 N. Beauregard St. • Alexandria, VA 22311-1714 USA
Telephone: 800-933-2723 or 703-578-9600 • Fax: 703-575-5400
Web site: http://www.ascd.org • E-mail: member@ascd.org

Gene R. Carter, *Executive Director;* Nancy Modrak, *Director of Publishing;*
Julie Houtz, *Director of Book Editing & Production;* Darcie Russell, *Project Manager;*
Judi Connelly, *Senior Graphic Designer;* Barton Matheson Willse & Worthington,
Typesetter; Tracey A. Smith, *Production Manager.*

Acknowledgments

I am humbled when I reflect on the many wonderful people who have contributed to my perspective and understanding of the issues addressed in this book.

At the top of my list is Donald Phillips, my 9th grade social studies teacher. It was he who inspired me to pursue a career in education and who, after more than 30 years in the classroom, is still inspiring his students to go forth and make a difference in the world.

My eyes were opened to how education can be a force for social change by Gertrud, Max, and Heinz Bondy, and the faculty of the Windsor Mountain School. They inspired me by their dedication to human rights and equity. From them I learned the importance of perseverance from their stalwart refusal to let racism, poverty, war, and even Nazism stand in the way of their commitment to human rights.

I want to thank my mentors. Professor Arthur Pearl's brilliance, passion, and fire are still pushing me to do all I can to make this a more equitable society. Dealous Cox, the wisest person I've ever met, showed me the power of transformational leadership and demonstrated how educators can support the conditions that enable others to achieve their full potential.

Above all else, this book is about optimism and I want to acknowledge those who instilled this in me through their actions and work. First among these are my parents, Harriet and Irving Sagor. Later, as my career unfolded, the research and dedication of Ron Edmonds, Wilbur Brookover, Larry Lezotte, and their colleagues in the Effective Schools Movement provided me with the armament I needed as an educator to never accept excuses for poor performance.

I am indebted to the students and teachers of the Bremerton, Washington, Alternative School for demonstrating the power of empowerment in my first years of teaching. I want to thank all the teachers and colleagues I've watched and learned from during my career. Special thanks go to Earl Down and the faculty at Creswell High School, Dave Campbell and the staff at South Umpqua High School, and all the incredibly creative and inspirational teachers at West Linn High School, for demonstrating to me what a teacher's hard work, professionalism, and dedication can mean for students.

My heartfelt gratitude goes to each of the teachers at the Camas School District who taught my daughters. Beginning on day one of kindergarten, these men and women have provided me with concrete proof of how school can be made CBUPO (Competence, Belonging, Usefulness, Potency, and Optimism) rich for students.

I want to doubly thank Bob Hamm for proofreading this manuscript and, more important, for demonstrating daily how a single language arts teacher can inspire joy and learning in students—even in areas where they had previously shown little or no interest.

It is hard to find the right words to express my feelings and thanks for the help of Joyce McLeod, my editor at the Association for Supervision and Curriculum Development. This kind, talented, and persistent woman has worked with my idiosyncrasies, guided me, and gently cajoled me into developing a work that I couldn't have done without her. Not only has my work with Joyce resulted in two books, but it has provided me with a new and valued friend.

Finally, I thank my wife, Tanis Knight. She deserves heaps of credit simply for being able to put up with me. But, more to the point of this work, she is an educator who continues to do good work and to inspire others to do good work, regardless of what obstacles are in her path. More than any other educator I know, Tanis graciously, quietly, and effectively walks her talk and for many years has made and is making a real difference for both teachers and students.

Motivating
Students & Teachers
in an Era of Standards

List of Figures and Implementation Strategies

Chapter 1

Identifying
Our Basic
Psychological Needs

Why do some students come to class motivated and ready to learn, while others seem completely uninterested? Why do some teachers count the days until retirement immediately after receiving tenure, and others are more energized in their 30th year of teaching than they were when they began? Are students and teachers capable of being excited by their involvement in education? Is it inevitable that the pursuit of standards will discourage and frustrate more teachers and students? If so, should society begin to brace itself for a greater number of dropouts and early retirements?

This chapter will respond to these questions and present a rationale for optimism. I firmly believe that every student and teacher can come to school each day and enter the classroom excited about the challenges ahead. I believe that educators can create environments where adults and youth arrive motivated to give their best effort. Furthermore, the result of the standards movement—for better or worse—is in the hands of everyone engaged in the education profession.

In many places, a focus on standards has already led, when managed one way, to increased student alienation and inflated dropout rates. Sadly, where this occurs, it disproportionately affects the more disadvantaged students—the very children who have the most to lose. But, when handled another way, the pursuit of tough and meaningful standards supplies just the tonic needed by all students, including those most at risk. Implemented purposefully and deliberately, standards can make the educational experience rewarding and exciting for every student.

The same possibilities hold true for teachers. Implementing standards-based reforms in one manner can result in reduced opportunities for teacher creativity, personal and professional growth, and the likelihood of gaining satisfaction from one's work. Such reforms can lead, and in some places already have led, to disastrous consequences. Often the people first to flee work that has lost its allure are the best and brightest—those who have the most options elsewhere. Worse, with the retirement of the baby boomers and an ever-increasing teacher shortage, those students in greatest need of inspired and excellent teaching—children in low-income communities—are being hurt the most. Yet, the greatest long-term impact of a demoralized profession is that teaching will become an even less attractive career option for the next generation of talented young people.

But the results of standards-based reforms need not be negative ones. Implemented in a different fashion, standards-based reform could be precisely what is needed to restructure teaching. Standards can bring teaching more in line with the other professions—those professions that consistently attract more talented applicants than the available positions can accommodate.

In this chapter, I will share why I am so optimistic. Then, in the following chapters, I will explore a series of specific strategies that you can implement to make high-powered education a positive experience for all your students, and the act of teaching a source of personal and professional satisfaction for yourself and your colleagues.

What Is Motivation?

What explains the polar opposites we see at school? Some kids are excited about learning, whereas others hate every minute of it. Some faculty members are energized and challenged by working with each new group of students, whereas others dread simply coming to work every day. Is this evidence of special virtues or fatal flaws? Has some sort of trauma made it impossible for some people to derive satisfaction from work in schools? Experience and research indicate that differences in motivation have less to do with individual personalities than with the way in which students and teachers experience the school environment.

What Does It Take to Motivate?

William Glasser (1998a, 1998b) did an excellent job of synthesizing the research on adult and youth motivation and reducing it to an easily understood metaphor. Glasser asserted that humans are born with a photo album in our psyche where we store life experiences. We keep those events that provoke feelings of pleasure in a particular section of this photo album, which Glasser labels a "quality world." Some of the early pictures in our photo albums remind us of the nurturing and unconditional love we received as infants. Later, Glasser asserted, as our lives unfold, we continue to seek opportunities to relive the type of events and experiences that appear in our quality world part of the album. Glasser broke down volumes of research on motivation into a finite set of feelings and needs that, he argued, are coveted by all humans. He said that whenever a particular experience satisfies at least one basic need, it is emotionally fulfilling and worthy of addition to the quality world photo album.

According to Glasser, the basic human needs are survival, freedom, power, fun, and belonging. I use different terms, but conceptually and functionally, the theory of motivation upon which this book is built is consistent with Glasser's theory. After reviewing the literature on human motivation, I found a way to summarize what innately motivates both youth and adults. To be motivated, people need to feel satisfied in the areas of

- Competence,
- Belonging,
- Usefulness,
- Potency, and
- Optimism.

So the question I posed earlier, Why are some people motivated by school and others are not?, can be answered with a simple response: If being a student or being a teacher provides a person with regular doses of feelings of competence, belonging, usefulness, and potency (CBUPs), then the person's quality world will fill up with images of those needs being satisfied at school. As a result, these students and teachers will look to school with optimism. They intuitively know that if they have always received CBUPs at school, then, in all likelihood, they will again. Once we add optimism (O) to the equation, we can summarize the phenomenon as follows:

> Motivated students or teachers are those who have received and anticipate receiving regular doses of CBUPOs from their experience at school.

The CBUPO Theory

The CBUPO theory explains why certain students and teachers are motivated: They receive regular doses of CBUPOs. It also provides a straightforward explanation of what needs to be done to motivate everyone else. When the school experience becomes CBUPO rich for those who now appear chronically unmotivated, their orientation to school will change. Unfortunately, just because a solution is simple to articulate (i.e., providing CBUPOs for all), that doesn't make it easy to achieve.

The Basic Need to Feel Competent

Our need to feel competent is satisfied when we have credible reason to believe that we are good at something. Furthermore, if the thing that we are proficient at is something valued by others, it becomes even more satisfying. Finally, if we believe that the things we are competent at are difficult and that our skills were developed through dedication and diligence, our sense of competence gets a greater boost.

The Student's Need for Feelings of Competence

The most motivated students are those whose participation at school has been accompanied by credible feedback on their skillfulness. Consequently, these students have internalized the direct relationship among perseverance, hard work, and success. The returns they receive on their investment of energy inevitably produce high self-esteem. This is the process that explains the truth in the saying "success breeds success."

For other students, those whose academic history has been filled with repeated evidence of shortcomings, the constant experience of failure has contributed to a belief that education as an endeavor simply makes one feel incompetent. Needless to say, incompetence is an emotional state most people choose to avoid.

For this reason, the challenge of motivating alienated students begins with a focus on finding authentic ways to increase opportunities for them to feel competent in the classroom. By giving students ways to feel competent, it becomes much more likely that they will learn what is necessary to be successful. In this way, students are able to experience the satisfaction of feeling competent.

Several practices have potential for making the experience of competency likely for all students. Teachers who use these practices systemically and deliberately are able to see once-alienated students develop enhanced feelings of personal competence. Strategies that produce competence include

- Student management of a portfolio of personal bests,
- Student monitoring of personal progress,
- Student involvement in the assessment of work, and
- Student demonstrations of proficiency on mandated standards.

Specific ways to implement these strategies will be discussed in depth in Chapter 2.

The Teacher's Need for Feelings of Competence

The circumstances that influence a student's feelings of competence are no different for the classroom teacher. Anyone who receives positive feedback on her work tends to see that work as a satisfying experience. It's not surprising that most coaches exhibit a high level of motivation. Why is it that they are so motivated to teach athletics to their students? A big part of their motivation comes from the performance of the athletes in competition and at practice. An athlete's performance provides the coach with concrete and irrefutable evidence of her teaching success. The coach knows that the athlete can now do something that he could not have done before. The only explanation for this growth in student skill is what the coach taught him and facilitated during practice, which is the coach's classroom.

Teachers of other subjects, those where students regularly produce products or present concrete performances demonstrating the value added by their teachers, often experience the type of motivation felt by a coach. For this reason, many teachers in the areas of music, art, drama, journalism, and vocational education are among the most motivated members of a school's faculty. These fortunate teachers receive daily feedback on their success in the practice of their chosen profession. Unfortunately, daily feedback is not a universal experience. Many teachers toil for what seems like endless hours, trying to stimulate student learning, yet on most days they leave school wondering, "Am I truly making any difference?"

Few teachers invest much faith in student scores on norm-referenced tests. Fewer believe that the written evaluations prepared by supervisors after two brief classroom observations provide a complete or credible report of their work. Consequently, many teachers work in a feedback vacuum. Not only do they receive little credible data on their success, but they hear on the news that they, collectively, have failed their students. The teachers who work in high-poverty schools have it even worse. For them, most often the school year ends with a report from the state or district telling them that their students—and by extension, they themselves—are low performing. This is hardly the stuff that builds feelings of competence.

To be truly motivated, all teachers must be given regular opportunities to validate the positive effects that their work is having on their students' lives. Having such opportunities ends the chronic need to ask whether teachers are truly making a difference, because the answer becomes evident and irrefutable for all who care to look. Teachers may receive validation by

- Altering the paradigm used for assessing student work, and

- Transforming the role of teacher from overseer to academic coach.

Chapter 2 explores strategies for incorporating these paradigms into the classroom.

The Basic Need to Feel Belonging

The feeling of belonging has two elements: comfort and acceptance. We are more inclined to experience belonging in environments where we feel comfortable. Feeling comfortable is analogous to how you feel when you are dressed in clothes that are becoming, fit well, and are suitable for the occasion. If you are dressed in clothes that don't fit or aren't appropriate, you will feel uncomfortable and wish you were anyplace else.

Feelings of acceptance result from our relationships with others. When people find themselves in a place that suits their sense of self and they are engaged with people they like and who enjoy being with them, they experience belonging. Conversely, when people are in an environment that appears strange and foreign, it reinforces their sense of being an outsider.

The Student's Need for Feelings of Belonging

Schools have been successful at providing some students with feelings of affiliation and belonging. There is good reason why motivated students use the possessive pronoun when they talk about *my* school, *my* class, or *my* team. It should be no surprise that students who feel comfortable and accepted at school tend to be those who are motivated to invest in their work and prosper academically. Unfortunately, a great many other students feel rejected by their classmates or experience other factors that cause them to feel out of place. Is it any wonder that these are the students who demonstrate the least commitment to the expectations of the school, their teachers, and the curricula?

Why do these differences persist? Often the classroom and school reward system—intentionally or unintentionally—favors certain students over others. One thing all students share is the belief that their school has a social hierarchy. They know the popular kids are on top, whereas others, those less highly regarded, are condemned to the bottom. When students suspect that they have been assigned to the latter group, it's no surprise that they tend to dislike going to school.

No one may be at fault. Teachers do not intend to make students feel alienated. Nevertheless, the consequences of certain unconscious teaching behaviors, when engaged in over and over, can do just that. For example, if the style of instruction employed by a teacher consistently conflicts with the cognitive strength or learning style of the student, it is unlikely the student will feel comfortable in class. Similarly, when students' families are culturally different from the mainstream (e.g., non-English proficient or from a minority culture), the students might not find aspects of their home culture at school. From the exclusion of familiar cultural practices, the students logically conclude their home culture isn't valued. Thus it is natural for a student in this situation to internalize the view that "people like me" are not accepted and consequently "do not belong here."

Teachers can have significant influence over elements of the social structure of their classrooms. Classroom governance procedures can cause students to experience their classroom as inclusive or exclusionary. The strategic use of particular instructional processes can serve to make our classrooms invitational to all the diverse learners who come through the classroom door. Making our schools and our classrooms culturally rich environments where multiculturalism is both embraced and valued helps many students to develop a deep sense of belonging.

Chapter 3 examines several strategies that can make our classrooms more inclusive and inviting for all students. The approaches that have been successful in making the school experience a source of belonging for everyone include

- Using classroom governance to promote affiliation,

- Making classrooms friendly to diverse learning styles, and

- Helping students appreciate and make productive use of cultural diversity.

The Teacher's Need for Feelings of Belonging

The classroom teacher's need for belonging is often overlooked in schools. Although this does not spring from evil design, it is the unintended result of a perspective that teachers are paid to do a job and it is up to them to make their work fulfilling. In addition, school administrators occasionally and incorrectly assume that because teachers are granted considerable autonomy within the walls of their classrooms, they don't have a professional need for collegiality and community.

In environments where workers have come to feel like members of high-performing teams and regularly get to enjoy the camaraderie of their coworkers, higher levels of performance are invariably produced (Senge, 1990; Senge et al., 1999). On the other hand, when the tasks that workers have to perform are challenging and perplexing and demand continuous creative problem solving, workers feel extremely frustrated when told to go it alone. For many teachers, the combination of working in isolation while being pushed to deliver universal student success becomes so frustrating that it leads to an unhealthy degree of stress, depression, and burnout. Studies by Little (1982) and McLaughlin and Talbert (2001) documented that the continued isolation of classroom teachers in this era of accountability and high expectations is a major contributing factor in the rising rate of teacher attrition. Society cannot afford to have public schools lose talented professionals simply because hostile work environments make it untenable for them. It is imperative that teaching be restructured into a more collaborative and collegial endeavor.

In Chapter 4, I present a set of practices that break down the isolation of teachers and create a sense of faculty as team. Specifically, we will examine mechanisms that foster collaboration and collegiality. There has never been a time when this has been more important because never before have the stakes been so high. Consider these two facts:

1. Nobody knows the complete answer to how a school can bring all students to proficiency on a set of difficult standards. I say this with confidence because I am unaware of that outcome ever being accomplished in

human history—even though it is now the stated policy in most jurisdictions.

2. It is the rare faculty where every teacher doesn't have some insight and hasn't developed some techniques that have succeeded with some students in the achievement of difficult standards.

When the insights of 30 to 50 members of a faculty are combined, the insight and innovation needed to realize universal success is far more likely to emerge. When this happens, members of the faculty can take justified pride in contributing to the group attainment of what once seemed an impossible task.

Just as we teachers can understand that group failure can breed group alienation, we should also recognize that success, when achieved as the result of teamwork, breeds profound feelings of pride.

The Basic Need to Feel Useful

Of the five basic motivational needs, feeling useful is one of the more crucial. Nothing feels as good as the knowledge that others need us and want our help. Our self-esteem gets a tremendous boost when we feel that others value our areas of strength as essential for their own success.

Conversely, when we feel that our work or skills lack value, that no one else's life would be affected much even if we ceased to exist, we are likely to internalize a sense of uselessness. When students and teachers experience school this way, they find little reason to care.

The Student's Need for Feelings of Usefulness

Schools provide many powerful opportunities for some students to feel useful. The student who plays first trumpet in band knows she will be missed if she doesn't make it to a performance. The spiker on the volleyball team knows her teammates are counting on her contribution to the team's success. The captain of the knowledge-bowl team knows that his insights are critical if the team is to prevail. And, the student body president likely thinks the success of the activity program rests completely on her shoulders. Yet, many other students don't see where or how their performance, or even their presence at school, makes much of a difference to anyone. When a student feels this way, it is logical for him to wonder why he should bother attending or working hard.

Teachers' actions and choices when deciding how to organize instruction can make the experience of usefulness a regular event for every student. The strategic use of cooperative learning can help students see their contributions to others' success. Experiencing problem-based learning and service learning helps students to gain proficiency with standards and also helps them to satisfy their basic need to feel useful.

Chapter 4 shares techniques for implementing cooperative learning, problem-based learning, and service learning in a way that ensures that all students have multiple chances to demonstrate proficiency on mandated standards while seeing the contribution their work is making to the well-being of others.

The Teacher's Need for Feelings of Usefulness

Perhaps never before has teacher self-esteem been more at risk. The media run stories about students lacking skills and schools that are failing; by inference, the story is that teachers are not meeting their obligations to the children. Vocal critics promote vouchers as a panacea because they conclude that public school teachers are incapable of meeting the challenges of educating today's youth. In many places, the annual ritual of front-page comparisons of scores on standardized tests is taken as a measure of the skill of a school's teaching staff. Some educators respond to this barrage of attacks by going on the attack themselves. The unprofitable blame game goes on far too frequently. High school faculties blame the middle schools; the middle schools blame the elementary schools; teachers blame parents and kids. Unions blame administrators, and administrators blame collective bargaining. All this blame serves no productive purpose.

Solutions to this spiraling problem exist. One is through the development of collaborative solutions to student learning needs, which will be examined in Chapter 3 where belonging is our focus. Another approach involves making better use of valid and reliable classroom-based assessment.

In chapters 2 and 4, we explore a process that teachers can use to accurately and reliably measure the contributions they personally make toward improved student performance. This process uses rate-of-growth and value-added measures rather than a total reliance on static normative and comparative statistics. The data that are produced via value-added assessment help all stakeholders—teachers, students, parents, schoolboard members, patrons—to appreciate and understand the contribution teachers make to student success.

The Basic Need for Feelings of Potency

When the goal is motivation, none of the four basic psychological needs is more important than the need to feel potent. Glasser refers to this as the need for power. When people have valid reasons to believe that they have influence over the factors that affect their ultimate success, they are more likely to exercise that influence. Conversely, if we hold doubt about our capacity to effect the changes necessary to improve our situation, it is understandable if we see little point in trying.

The Student's Need for Feelings of Potency

Motivated, high-performing students often take credit for their success. When they do this, it is not necessarily braggadocio, nor should teachers find it problematic. Rather, teachers should see it as evidence that students recognize that their actions and choices led to their successes. The adage "If you think you can, you can, but, if you think you can't, you can't" couldn't be more appropriate for today's students.

In the current era of standards, the consequences of school failure will be a life sentence for many students. Failing to meet a standard severely limits a student's opportunities in the future. If students leave classes feeling that they have no power or influence over their ultimate success or if they conclude that failure is inevitable, they possess no justification to invest in turning things around. In some cases, the young person's feelings of impotence leads her to search for instant gratification and immediate success through behavior that requires little effort, and can prove quite self-destructive. Teachers shouldn't be surprised to find that students who possess an external locus of control (i.e., have the belief that others control their future) are those most likely to end up involved with drugs and engaged in criminal activity.

In Chapter 5, I will examine a set of proven strategies that build student feelings of personal power, or potency. Specifically, we will explore how an internal locus of control can be developed and strengthened through the deliberate and strategic use of good classroom management practices.

The Teacher's Need for Feelings of Potency

For teachers, the need for feelings of potency is closely aligned with their need for feelings of usefulness. Given the numerous social and economic factors that today's students grapple with, many teachers probably suspect that their own power and ability to influence student performance and behavior is limited. Many teachers have heard colleagues saying, "Let's be realistic. There is only so much *one* teacher can do!"

Although that sentiment is understandable, it breeds enormous problems. Teachers who feel that their contributions are severely limited have good reason to give their work less than a full measure of effort. More important, teachers who feel this way are devaluing their personal worth. Of course, the consequences for the students taught by such teachers are even worse. If teachers doubt that they have the power to influence improvement in student performance, the chances for student success are slim indeed.

To change this feeling of impotency requires a concerted effort to make the nuts and bolts of educational reform a local matter. When teachers see reform as something being done to them by the state or worked out at the district office, it only reinforces their sense of impotence. However, if teachers see that the reform effort (i.e., helping more students achieve success) is built on their creative and collective ability to design novel and promising approaches to perplexing educational problems, then their sense of potency will be reinforced.

Optimism

Please note that the four feelings of competence, belonging, usefulness, and potency are not independent or discrete phenomena. The satisfaction of one need frequently has a positive spillover effect that helps satisfy another. Figure 1.1 visually displays the dynamic relationship between the satisfaction of these four needs.

Given the interactive relationship of the four basic human emotional needs (competence, belonging, usefulness, and potency), teachers must focus on satisfying all the needs simultaneously. The positive effects of spillover (from one emotional need to another) should be expected and appreciated.

In Chapter 6, I will look at strategies that help teachers succeed in institutionalizing optimism and encourage them to use their unique and creative problem-solving abilities. I will examine methods that schools have implemented to help faculty teams

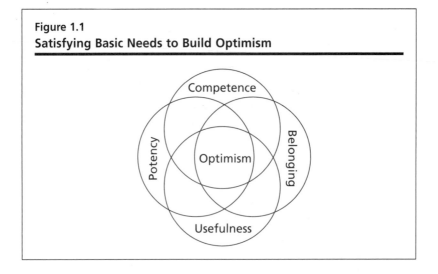

Figure 1.1
Satisfying Basic Needs to Build Optimism

be more successful and to acknowledge and celebrate a teaching team's collective role in successfully overcoming what once seemed insurmountable obstacles.

Student's Need for Optimism

Optimism refers to the personal vision that students hold regarding their future. Intuitively, people believe the best predictor of the future is the past. This is why students who have experienced CBUPs regularly at school logically anticipate receiving CBUPs in the future. Conversely, students who have consistently left school feeling incompetent, alienated, useless, and impotent expect their future endeavors to contain more of the same.

Occasionally, even students who have received ample doses of CBUPs hold a pessimistic view of their future. As significant people in their lives, teachers can assist them in the discovery of legitimate reasons for optimism. Several ways to promote students' feelings of optimism can be found in the concluding chapter of this book.

The Teacher's Need for Optimism

It is not just students who have a need to become optimistic. Teachers also need to believe. It is reasonable for teachers to worry about what is around the bend. As education has increasingly become a political game, teachers have many reasons for insecurity. But this insecurity can be lessened if teachers, individually and as a team, consistently receive CBUPs from their work. With repeated experiences that provide teachers with credible evidence that they are good (competent), that they are part of a quality team (belong), that they have the capacity to make a critical difference in students' lives (useful), and that they have the power (potency) to overcome whatever comes up, then the uncertainties of the future will become far less fearsome.

For students and teachers to individually experience CBUPs on a regular basis is critical, but it is also important that entire schools do what they can to institutionalize optimism as part of the professional culture of the workplace. This process is addressed in Chapter 6.

Chapter 2

Creating a Meaningful Sense of Competence

Much to our dismay as teachers, many students do not see us as allies. To these students the teacher is an adversary, a force to be overcome, or at the minimum, a force to negotiate with. In their book *The Shopping Mall High School,* Arthur Powell, Eleanor Farrar, and David Cohen (1985) described the student-teacher relationship as one that begins with the negotiation of a peace treaty. The students do their best to persuade teachers to lower their expectations, and the teacher attempts to nudge the students to do as much work as possible. Ultimately, both sides compromise on some middle ground.

Although the negotiation of treaties can make a classroom more harmonious, it also creates two significant problems:

1. If the goal is to help students experience true feelings of competence, it is necessary for them to succeed in meeting or exceeding high expectations. Simply demonstrating that one is capable of accomplishing a minimum doesn't cause one to feel skillful.

2. In most jurisdictions, schools and students face standards that are nonnegotiable. The teacher doesn't have the authority to lower the bar. Furthermore, the

expectation in most states and provinces is for students to perform at high levels of proficiency, not just demonstrate competency.

The Difference Between the Classroom and the Athletic Field

Teachers can meet the challenge that the standards movement calls for, but to do so requires a major change in the prevailing student-teacher relationship. Fortunately, a prototype relationship exists within the school environment. For example, though many students see their classroom teacher as an adversary, they don't necessarily have that type of relationship with all other adults in the school. In extracurricular activities such as music, drama, and athletics, the adult-student relationship is based on a fundamentally different premise. Young athletes and performers begin the relationship with their coach or director knowing that their own goals and the coach's or director's goals are one and the same. Both adults and youth share a commitment to achieving a victory or producing an award-winning performance. Additionally, the criteria that determine success are not controlled by the teacher. Rules, scoring criteria, or the preparation of the opposing team determine success for an athlete or a performer. The external nature of the criteria or circumstances that influence success may be the most significant feature that distinguishes performance activities from those usually demanded in the classroom. The athlete or performer sees little purpose in expending energy to try to persuade the coach or director to lower the success criteria. In addition, student athletes and performers know that the coach (their teacher) covets victory as much as they do, so it is counterproductive to work against one another.

Knowledge Workers and Academic Coaches

Recognizing the difference between the athlete-coach relationship and how students tend to perceive the teacher-student relationship has led many thoughtful educators to suggest a profound paradigm shift, one that transforms the job descriptions of both teacher and student (Sizer, 1992). In this new paradigm, the teacher becomes an "academic coach" and the student takes on the role of a "knowledge worker."

I have come to understand these new relationships by comparing it with the relationship among construction workers and their supervisor. It is the workers' job to do the work. For example, the workers build the bridge or construct the house. When the project is successfully completed, the workers can stand back and admire the fruits of their labor, and each can take pride in what was accomplished. Although it is the workers' job to do the work, it is the supervisor's job to assist (coach) the workers so that they can do their job in an excellent fashion.

It is essential that we educators adopt the worker-supervisor (knowledge worker-academic coach) model if we hope to build student competence in a standards-based world. As in athletics and the competitive work world, others set the criteria for success. Education ministries or departments of education set the standards, and they will continue to be set high. Furthermore, in a standards-based system, as in athletics, the arts, and in any profession, continuous success and improvement can only be achieved as a result of hard work and perseverance.

In education, knowledge workers and their academic coaches can readily agree that it is the knowledge worker's job to execute the work (the acquisition of knowledge and skill). After all, it is the knowledge workers who perform on the state exam, the SAT, or at an interview with a potential employer. In the knowledge worker-academic coach paradigm, students heading off to school have the same mindset as adults going to their workplace. Students know that their job description is the acquisition of knowledge and skills. But, they also know they are not alone; an academic coach is available to help them.

At the academic job site, high-quality supervisors have been provided solely for the knowledge workers' benefit. The folks who supervise the knowledge workers have the same job description as supervisors in the adult workplace: to provide assistance to the workers so they can get the work done well.

This relationship parallels that of the coach and athlete. For example, on Monday both coach and athlete agree on a goal: to score a perfect 10 in Friday's diving competition. In the classroom, the knowledge worker and academic coach might also agree on a goal the first day of class (academic practice): to do an outstanding job on the state test to be given on April 15. As the athletes proceed through the weekly regimen of tough practices, good coaches regularly communicate that they are there to do everything in their power to prepare the players for competition. However, the coaches also let it be known that it is the players' job to put forth the necessary effort during practice. Similarly, in class, teachers (the academic coaches) must tell their students, "Although the state standards have been set high, we have confidence that you will be able to meet them and excel." Furthermore, we teachers should let the students know that we are prepared to do whatever it takes to assist them in gaining the necessary skills. But, the students also need to realize that success is ultimately determined by their willingness to put forth their best efforts.

Adopting the Knowledge Worker- Academic Coach Paradigm in the Classroom

The shift to the new paradigm begins with rethinking the prevailing approach to assessment that has become fashionable in this era of standards.

Rate-of-Growth Assessment Versus Normative Assessment

Normative assessment is the evaluation of student performance by comparing students with their age-mates. Another use of normative assessment is to evaluate a school's performance by comparing the scores achieved by students at one school with the scores obtained by students at other schools. Everyone knows this annual ritual. On a specified date each spring, the results of the state or provincial test are posted on the department of education's Web site and are released to the press. The next day, teachers awake to a morning paper containing a rank-ordered list of the scores received by local schools. Everyone knows well that the first thing parents, students, and teachers do is to scan the list to see where their local school ranks. If the school is high on the list, everyone breathes a sigh of relief and may even bask in glory for the next 12 months.

As teachers, we have all witnessed a similar situation at parent conferences. The parent asks, "How well is Jeffrey doing compared with his classmates?" If Jeffery is "above grade level," his parent is satisfied. However, should he be performing below his peers, his parent may logically become concerned.

Once the test scores have been released, schools that performed low and the students who posted scores below grade level are admonished to work harder and increase the priority they are giving to the objectives measured by the test. This directive is based upon an assumption that if the faculty and the students were willing to work hard enough, next year's results will move them up in the rankings. A higher ranking is important to educators because such an outcome is seen as vindicating the quality of the school and the teaching. Unfortunately, more often than not, the schools that ranked low one year will rank low the following year.

Predictably, when a school remains low in the rankings, the voices of the critics become shrill. They ask "Why is this school always so far below the state average? Why don't they improve? Don't these teachers care about the kids?" In reality, the teachers and the students at the low-performing schools could be working diligently at improvement. Why then don't the test results reflect this?

Normative data can be misleading

Evaluating student performance only by comparing students to their age-mates can be misleading for the following reasons:

■ Frequently, low-performing schools serve low-income communities. For a variety of reasons, family income is the best predictor of performance on standardized tests. Furthermore, families in low-income communities tend to move a great deal, resulting in greater student transiency in low-income schools.

Consequently, many of the children who are tested and whose scores are reported may have spent little time at the school. If a great many students who took the test didn't actually attend the school, their scores cannot be fairly used as an indicator of school quality.

■ Most state or provincial testing programs report changes in performance by grade level. Therefore, when the state or newspaper reports on changes from year one to year two, often they aren't comparing the same kids. Instead they are comparing this year's 4th graders to last year's 4th graders. You don't need to be a statistician to realize this amounts to comparing apples with oranges. Perhaps the kids who were in last year's 4th grade learned a great deal and their skills improved dramatically, but an assessment system that doesn't track the same students cannot capture these trends.

■ The lowest-performing schools often find themselves far behind the high-performing schools. If a school or a student is scoring in the 20th percentile, which would translate as several years below grade level, it isn't realistic to expect all of that ground to be made up in one year. In most high-achieving schools, the students are expected to demonstrate one year's growth in one year's time. Given that fact, is it fair to expect more disadvantaged children to grow 3 or 4 grade levels in the same time frame?

Is it any wonder that the teachers and students who are criticized continuously for being at the bottom of the heap stop trying? Should we be surprised when teachers who are consistently berated because their students do not achieve at the same level as students of other teachers begin to feel something less than competent? And how many times do students need to be told they are scoring in the bottom quartile before they conclude they just can't learn?

Another way to interpret data

The negative effects of normative assessment needn't be the case, and the solution won't require us to change state or provincial policy. However, what it will require is reporting the same test data in an additional way—a method known as rate-of-growth assessment. To increase the value of test data, the scores need to be used to answer three essential questions:

1. Are the students in our program developing the knowledge and skill that they need?

2. How fast are the students acquiring the needed knowledge and skill?

3. Is this rate-of-growth satisfactory to allow our lower-performing students to catch up to their higher-achieving peers?

Let's assume I am coaching a 7th grade girl who tells me her goal is to play basketball at the collegiate level. She asks me for a realistic appraisal of her performance. Do I tell her that she is not as good as most of the college players I've seen? Of course not! Why would I expect a 7th grader to perform like a collegiate athlete? Instead, I tell her the degree of improvement she needs to make over the next 5 years to reach the level of performance expected of a college athlete. If she has been doing a good job of developing her skills, I might say, "In my opinion, if you keep improving at your current rate, I am sure you will meet your goal."

As another example, when NASA sends a probe to explore Jupiter—a trip that takes many years—does it call the space shot a failure because after just six months it hasn't passed Jupiter? No way! NASA is delighted to say, "Our probe is right on track. If it maintains this trajectory for six more years, it will pass by Jupiter right on schedule."

To bring this discussion back to education, review the performance of students at two schools on a standardized 6th grade test (see Figure 2.1). At School A, students are achieving at a level that, if maintained until 12th grade, will qualify these students to matriculate at the state university. If the goal is to have all its students eligible to pursue a four-year degree, the students simply need to maintain their current level of performance (i.e., one year's growth in one year's time). At School B, the students are performing well below grade level. In fact, the average performance at this school is a full 3 years below where it should be.

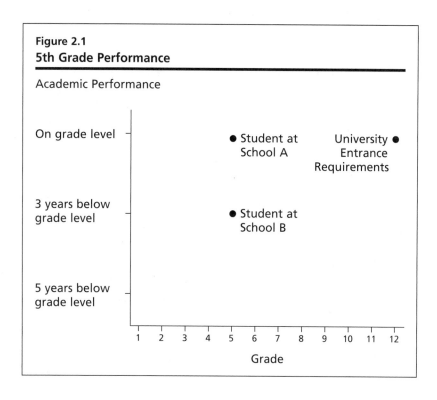

Figure 2.1
5th Grade Performance

If people expect School B to catch School A in one year, they will be disappointed. But, why should that be the goal? Assume the aspirations of students and parents at School B are the same as those of the students attending School A: "We want to be eligible to attend a four-year university where we can pursue our chosen careers." Although that is not an inappropriate goal for the students at School B, it is critical for them to take stock of what is necessary to get there. Figure 2.2 illustrates the rate of growth that must be attained by the students at these two schools if they are to achieve the same goal.

Now imagine that the teachers and students at School B demonstrate growth at a rate necessary to meet their goal (i.e., eligibility to attend a four-year university). How will their performance look at the end of the 7th grade in comparison to their counterparts attending School A? Not very good. The newspapers will report that the students attending School B are continuing to perform well below grade level and they are still miles

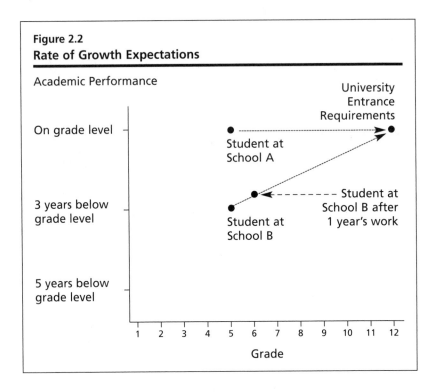

Figure 2.2
Rate of Growth Expectations

away from their higher-achieving counterparts. Although that is true, does it really matter? Let's now reinterpret the same data, but use them to answer the three key questions posed earlier.

1. Are the students in our program developing the knowledge and skills that they need?

Definitely. Their improvement from the year before is ample evidence of that.

2. How fast are the students acquiring the needed knowledge and skill?

They are acquiring skills at a rate of 1.5 year's growth in one year's time, a rate that is 50 percent faster than is being achieved at the higher-performing school.

3. Is this rate of growth satisfactory to allow our students to catch up to their higher achieving peers?

Yes. If they maintain this rate of growth, they will catch up by the end of 12th grade, just in time to enter the university.

When the data are interpreted this way, both students and teachers should experience well-deserved feelings of competence. Furthermore, the trend shown by these data provides motivation to both students and teachers to keep plugging away. After all, the teachers in School B are adding value at a rate 50 percent faster than the teachers at School A.

What is especially good about rate-of-growth assessment is that it is easily understood by students, parents, teachers, and policy makers and is a more honest reflection of school and student improvement than is pure normative assessment. As helpful as rate-of-growth assessment is, it is unrealistic and inadvisable to wait 12 months to find out how fast students are improving. Teachers and students need more immediate feedback if they are to feel competent and continue working hard at their jobs as knowledge workers and academic coaches. Fortunately, it isn't necessary to wait 12 months to report to students on their rate of growth. Figure 2.3 contains a list of the number, operation, and quantitative reasoning objectives that are expected of 6th graders in Texas. A school might keep this type of listing in each student's math portfolio.

Now let's assume that I'm teaching 6th grade in Texas, it is September, and after pretesting I notice that Yolanda is proficient

---

Figure 2.3
Essential Knowledge and Skills for Grade 6 Mathematics (Texas)

Number, operation, and quantitative reasoning. The student adds, subtracts, multiplies, and divides to solve meaningful problems.

The student is expected to

(A) Use addition and subtraction to solve problems involving whole numbers and decimals;
(B) Use multiplication to solve problems involving whole numbers (no more than three digits times two digits without technology);
(C) Use division to solve problems involving whole numbers (no more than two-digit divisors and three-digit dividends without technology);
(D) Identify prime factors of a whole number and common factors of a set of whole numbers; and
(E) Model and record addition and subtraction of fractions with like denominators in problem-solving situations.

on all the 5th grade objectives. However, she has yet to master any of the skills assigned to 6th grade. The state assessment is to be given at the end of April, and my students need to show proficiency on 16 discrete skills by that time. To help my students monitor their own progress, I would create a tracking form that is kept in each student's math portfolio (see Figure 2.4).

If Yolanda is to demonstrate proficiency on the April assessment, she needs to master the 6th grade objectives at a rate of two per month. As she records her progress on the tracking form, she can see visual evidence of her rate of progress. Better yet, if she continues to show growth at a rate of at least two standards per month, she can feel confident that she is right on track to meet her goal.

Developing mileposts on the road to standard mastery

When I'm driving on the highway, I can tell how well I am advancing toward my destination by the rate at which I pass mile markers. When teachers provide students with milepost markers along their path to mastery, both student and teacher can chart their progress and take pride in their growth.

Implementation Strategy 2.1 is designed to help a teaching team construct mileposts that they and their students can use to monitor continuous progress.

Implementation Strategy 2.1

Constructing Mileposts to Measure Teaching and Learning Success

Step 1. Review the Standards

Meet with colleagues to review those standards that the state or district expects to be accomplished at your grade level. In states or provinces that have developed their own mandated testing programs, a state or ministry publication delineating the standards should contain all the information needed for this meeting. In states or provinces that have adopted a standardized test for assessment, a test manual available from the publisher will accomplish the same purpose.

Figure 2.4
Math Tracking Sheet—
Number, Operation, and Quantitative Reasoning

Use a tracking sheet for each student and insert the date each standard is achieved to track progress.

Date	Standard
	Use addition to solve problems involving whole numbers
	Use subtraction to solve problems involving whole numbers
	Use addition to solve problems involving decimals
	Use subtraction to solve problems involving decimals
	Use multiplication to solve problems (one digit times one digit)
	Use multiplication to solve problems (one digit times two digits)
	Use multiplication to solve problems (two digits times two digits)
	Use multiplication to solve problems (two digits times three digits)
	Use division to solve problems (one digit divided by one digit)
	Use division to solve problems (two digits divided by one digit)
	Use division to solve problems (two digits divided by two digits)
	Use division to solve problems (three digits divided by two digits)
	Identify prime factors of a whole number
	Identify common factors of a set of whole numbers
	Model and record addition of fractions with like denominators in problem-solving situations
	Model and record subtraction of fractions with like denominators in problem-solving situations

Use a graph as a visual tool to show each student's progress toward meeting the standards. Color one column for each standard as it is achieved; adapt the units of time to match your school schedule.

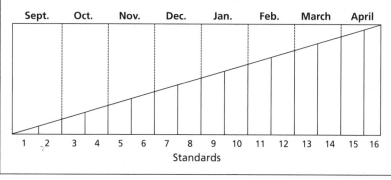

Step 2. Clarify the Targets

If sample test items are available, these should be reviewed. If sample items are not available, the group should ask itself, "What would we want a proficient example of student work on this standard to look like?"

Step 3. Develop a Prompt

Ask, "What is an assignment or prompt teachers could use to elicit the type of student work identified in Step 2?"

Step 4. Gather Data

Administer the assignment or prompt and review the work produced.

Step 5. Identify Range

Each teacher should select two samples: (1) illustrative of the weakest work submitted, and (2) illustrative of work that met or exceeded proficiency as determined in Step 2.

Step 6. Identify Possible Traits

Each teacher compares the two pieces of work and tries to answer this question: "What critical aspects (traits or skills) of the work that demonstrated proficiency were superior to those found in the weak piece of work?"

Step 7. Agree on Traits

Collect the lists of critical aspects that were identified. Then work as a group to reach consensus on a set of critical traits or skills that need to be present in a piece of work that demonstrates mastery of the standard.

Step 8. Create Mileposts

For each trait or skill, brainstorm a sequential list of mileposts that students would need to pass on the road to mastery if they were traveling from the weakest possible performance to a level that met or exceeded the standard. Figure 2.5 shows mileposts, arranged by four traits, that students might need to pass on the route to proficiency within the skill of problem solving.

Step 9. Monitor Progress

Students produce work samples on a regular basis and record the mileposts as they pass them.

Step 10. Acknowledge and Celebrate

Celebrate the distance your students have traveled. Remind yourself that every milepost passed is concrete evidence of the value that you (the academic coach) have added to that student's growth and development. Students should also be encouraged to take pride in their progress along the road to mastery.

Note: A strategy worth using when dealing with significant student transiency is to arrange for entry and exit assessments for each student on each standard. A comparison of these two performances is concrete evidence of what was gained during the time the student was in your class.

Figure 2.5
Problem-Solving Skills

This is a sample list of the mileposts students might need to pass on the route to problem solving proficiency.

Focusing, Attending, and Remembering
- brainstorming
- accessing prior knowledge
- setting purpose
- attending to specific information
- recalling
- retelling
- organizing thoughts
- rehearsing
- engaging in active listening
- gathering information

Integrating Information
- predicting and confirming
- questioning
- making connections
- summarizing
- drawing conclusions
- using textual references
- extending ideas

Analyzing and Organizing
- identifying attributes
- comparing and contrasting
- identifying main ideas, setting, events, and roles of main characters
- classifying
- sequencing
- recording information
- outlining
- identifying gaps

Elaborating, Evaluating, and Reflecting
- discussing
- explaining
- extending ideas
- inferring
- describing
- justifying
- sorting essential and nonessential information
- establishing criteria
- self-questioning
- giving feedback
- clarifying information and ideas
- drawing conclusions

The Goal Setting–Achieving–Celebrating Cycle

In athletics, two concepts have demonstrated significant motivational value:

1. The goal setting–affirming–achieving–celebrating cycle, and
2. Regular assessment and acknowledgment of personal bests.

Coaches often have their athletes publicly affirm their personal goals prior to each competition. On Monday evenings in the fall, the lockers of football players are often adorned with statements such as

- I will make five unassisted tackles,
- I will rush for more than 75 yards, and
- I will complete more than 50 percent of my passes.

Every day at practice that week, the athlete is expected to work diligently in an effort to achieve these personal goals. Then on Friday night, after the game, the team meets in the locker room and data on each player's achievements are reviewed. When goals are achieved, the entire team celebrates and the player is awarded a decal that is proudly worn on the helmet for the remainder of the season. When an athlete's performance does not meet the goal, the same goal is affirmed for the following week.

Let's now take a look at Implementation Strategy 2.2. It provides a four-step process designed to adapt the goal cycle to the academic classroom.

Implementation Strategy 2.2

Identifying the Goal Cycle in the Academic Classroom

Step 1. Articulating Goals

Early in the school year, the academic coach (the teacher) should clearly outline for the students what expectations the school, the state, and their coach have established for them. These are the standards of performance that students are required to meet and demonstrate by the end-of-year assessment. At this point, you should give students the following information:

■ The state standards that have been assigned to this grade level,

■ The skills that will be assessed on the final exam,

■ The district's promotion and graduation standards, and

■ Your goals for their learning.

In the end, it will be up to the students themselves to decide whether they will accept these goals as their own. However, before I ask them to commit, I do my best to articulate the rationale and value of making the achievement of these goals a priority.

Step 2. Affirming Goals

The students are asked to reflect and publicly affirm their own goals or their personal vision of what they want to accomplish over a specified period of time (e.g., the end of the semester, the conclusion of the school year, in time for graduation). In most cases, students incorporate the external expectations, as shared by the teacher, into their goal statements. Should they elect not to, it is your job as academic coach to require that the knowledge workers understand the ramifications of not committing to the external expectations (e.g., failure to graduate and restricted future opportunities).

When older students affirm their goals, it is helpful to use a form such as the one displayed in Figure 2.6. With younger students, it is often best to have the affirmations shared orally in a conference with the teacher or a classroom aide who later puts them in written form.

Step 3. Preparing a Plan of Action

Knowledge workers next plot out a viable strategy, or work plan, for the achievement of their personal goals. In the old teacher-directed paradigm, it was entirely the teacher's job to find or design all the specific strategies or mechanisms that would guide student learning. Teachers called these lesson plans. Unfortunately, when teachers take on total responsibility for planning the learning and students

---

Figure 2.6
Goal Affirmation Sheet

Name: _____ Date: _____ Class: _____

Have you reviewed the departmental goals for this class?

Yes _____ No _____ N/A _____

Have you reviewed the state standards assigned to this class?

Yes _____ No _____ N/A _____

If you answered yes, please attach a copy of those goals and standards. If you answered no, please review the goals and standards before proceeding.

What would you like to accomplish as a result of your work in this class? When do you expect to have this accomplished?

_____

_____

_____

_____

_____

If you choose not to make the achievement of course goals or attainment of standards part of your goals (above), please explain why.

_____

_____

_____

_____

_____   _____
Student Signature   Parent or Guardian Signature

---

aren't successful, students tend to blame their failure on their teachers. How many times have you heard students saying "Don't blame me, it's not my fault. This teacher doesn't know what she's doing!" or "How did he expect me to do it right when he didn't explain it correctly!"

In the new paradigm, where the teacher is the academic coach and the student is the knowledge worker, different roles are assumed in the design of the learning. In the new model, the knowledge workers are expected to clearly and sequentially detail everything that they assume or believe needs to occur to achieve the goals. For example, if a 3rd grader's goal is to independently read chapter books by the end of the year, the student might theorize the following strategy:

- Read for 20 minutes each night,

- Practice retelling every story I've read to an adult, and

- Ask my teacher or media specialist to recommend books for me to read that are at the right level of difficulty for me.

The student may outline the first draft of a plan on a form (see Figure 2.7) or by drawing a flowchart (see Figure 2.8).

Once students have completed the first draft of their plans, they share it at a conference with the teacher and parent. When called for, the academic coach offers suggestions or revisions for consideration by the knowledge worker. The

---

Figure 2.7
Sample Plan for Developing Skills

Name: Jody Smith   Date: Sept. 15, 2002   Class: Mr. Sagor, Rm 24

What is the goal you want to achieve?
I want to be able to independently read chapter books by the end of 3rd grade.

What things will you need to do to meet your goal?
1. Meet with Ms. Richards each week to get book recommendations.
2. Check out a recommended book from the library.
3. Read to myself for at least 20 minutes each night.
4. Retell what I read tonight and summarize what came earlier in the book to Mom or Dad.
5. Keep a log of my reading every night and write a summary of what I read.
6. Share my log with my teacher every Friday and with Ms. Richards every Monday during the library period.
7. Ask my teacher to evaluate my reading at least once every month.

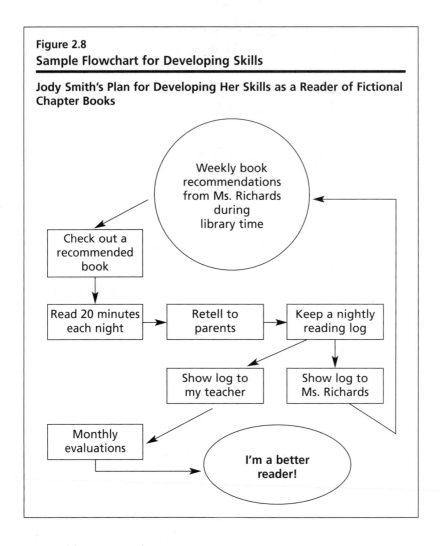

Figure 2.8
Sample Flowchart for Developing Skills

Jody Smith's Plan for Developing Her Skills as a Reader of Fictional Chapter Books

knowledge worker generally recognizes that the coach's suggestions are worth considering, if for no other reason than the coach's experience with helping other knowledge workers attain the same goal. This is analogous to athletes justifying the attention they give to their coach's direction with the argument, "I do what he says because he's been there."

Step 4. Coaching the Knowledge Worker

Once the knowledge worker has drafted and committed to a work plan that the coach agrees is a realistic approach to achieving the goal, both student and teacher move into high gear. It becomes the job of the knowledge worker to carry out the plan, whereas the job of the academic coach transitions to providing assistance as the plan is executed. For the teacher, assistance primarily means monitoring and providing timely and helpful feedback, which differs from the traditional paradigm in which the teacher spends most of her time engaged in direct instruction.

Regularly engaging in activities such as reviewing the student's reading log, reviewing the portfolio, paraphrasing responses to questions, assessing work samples, and holding informal conferences are among the ways coaches help knowledge workers ascertain whether they are making progress toward the achievement of their goals.

Step 5. Reporting and Reviewing Results

Once the plan has been carried out, the academic coach schedules a meeting with the knowledge worker to review the implementation of the work plan and whatever growth has been demonstrated. The meeting can be a student-led parent conference, a public presentation of a student portfolio, or a written self-assessment. Whatever reporting process is used, it is important that the knowledge worker's report respond to these four questions:

1. What was my goal?
2. What did I believe I needed to do to achieve my goal?
3. What did I do?
4. What were the results?

When the students are successful in attaining their goals, they can take personal credit for the achievement. Most often, successful results occur if students developed explicit goals and teachers assisted them in the development and timely execution of a viable work plan. Using this approach, the young knowledge workers will not be able to denigrate their success with comments such as "The test was easy," or "My teacher liked me."

Step 6. Taking Stock

When success is achieved, students know that it is because they did a good job executing the plans that they developed. Following the four-step process to implement the goal cycle assists students in seeing themselves as competent, perhaps even excellent, knowledge workers.

On the rare occasion when students fail to achieve success despite clear goals, a logical plan, and timely and positive coaching, it is usually the result of choices by the students to deviate from their own plans. Although such occurrences may not support the students' feelings of competence, it forces them to take responsibility for their decisions. This, in itself, teaches an important motivational lesson. The students who did not follow their work plan learn that problems such as irresponsibility and failure to follow through are also traits that they have the power to change. Helping students realize the power they have to alter behavior patterns that they see as counterproductive is discussed in Chapter 5.

The Concept of Personal Best

When I was a high school principal in western Oregon, I marveled each spring at what seemed, at least on the surface, to be rather bizarre behavior. I wondered what would cause a rational adult to coach track and field. Even stranger, I thought, was the behavior of the athletes who went out for track. I say this because it rains all spring in western Oregon. Every afternoon, a 3-hour practice is held on a wet, muddy field. After practice, both athletes and coaches enter the locker room, cold and wet and looking like drowned rats. Add to that a lack of glory—at our school, more people were judging the events than were attending as spectators. Furthermore, the local paper gave almost no ink to the exploits of our runners and jumpers.

Not only was it unlikely that our team would win a championship, but most of the kids wouldn't even compete at the varsity level. Why, then, were these otherwise rational people engaged in what seemed to be such an unpleasant activity? I came to understand their motivation when I posed two rhetorical questions (Sagor, 1991):

1. How long would a coach continue to work in the rain with kids who weren't likely to bring glory to the team, if one thing were changed: the use of the stopwatch and measuring tape would be banned at practice?

2. How long would teenagers voluntarily give up 3 hours a day to work out in the cold and rain without any chance of basking in the spotlight if they weren't regularly timed and measured?

I realized the answer to my questions was, "Not for very long. The use of measuring tools was essential." Every day, members of the track team could go into the warm, dry locker room after practice, armed with concrete evidence that their hard work made a difference. Indeed, they had credible data that they were now running faster or jumping higher than before. Each night the coaches had evidence of the growth they were helping their athletes develop. It became clear to me that this continuous measurement and assessment process was the best explanation for their perseverance. Every second shaved off an athlete's time was evidence to the coach that the kid was competent. Every personal best achieved by the athletes was proof that they were getting better.

Personal Bests in the Classroom

Several years ago, the brokerage firm Dean Witter ran an extraordinarily successful advertising campaign. It featured the founder of the company declaring, "At Dean Witter we measure success one investor at a time."

The same motto should apply to us as athletic and academic coaches. If we want our jobs to supply us with feelings of competence, then we need to collect data and assess our work one student at a time. Although there are many good reasons to encourage the use of student portfolios, using them to provide irrefutable documentation for both learner and teacher on continuous student development is the most compelling.

Implementation Strategy 2.3 builds on the goal cycle outlined in Implementation Strategy 2.2, and provides motivational benefits for students as well as teachers. In addition, it can help build parental support.

Implementation Strategy 2.3

Building and Sharing a Portfolio of Personal Bests

Step 1. Affirm Goals

Have your students develop and affirm their academic goals, making use of the goal setting process in Implementation Strategy 2.2. The goals that emerge become the first item in a student's portfolio of personal bests (see Figure 2.6, p. 32).

Step 2. Outline a Plan

Have the students write a narrative or draw a web illustrating their plan for achieving these academic goals. The work plans that emerge become the second item in the portfolio of personal bests (see examples in figures 2.7, p. 33 and 2.8, p. 34).

Step 3. Assess the Plan

Ask the student the following question, "If you follow your plan, how will you know it is working? What evidence will be produced along the way to demonstrate your progress?" The answer to this question becomes the student's assessment plan.

Step 4. Monitor Progress

Confer with all students to help them develop a list of performances that would constitute evidence of what they achieved. Examples students might suggest include weekly spelling quizzes, final drafts of essays, or unit tests.

Step 5. Assemble the Portfolio

Each item on the list becomes a section in the portfolios. The students insert the first piece of work they did this year into the appropriate section. They then proceed to add each and every piece of work deemed better than their previous personal best. Whenever a piece of work is placed in the portfolio, students append a statement explaining what made this piece of work better than what had been done previously. See Figure 2.9 for an example of a form that can be used for this purpose.

Step 6. Report Progress

Arrange for students to share the portfolios with their parents or guardians. An excellent way to accomplish this experience in the elementary grades is through a student-led parent-teacher conference. For secondary students, an end-of-year exhibition presented before the class, with parents invited, is a good approach. Another strategy is to ask the students to conduct a conference at home with their parents. The format of such a conference is determined by a teacher-generated agenda, and the students are required to write a summary of the conference. The student and parent should sign the summary.

For students and teachers to willingly invest their finite energy into the accomplishment of high-level objectives, they must have confidence in themselves. They need to believe in the depths of

---

Figure 2.9
Portfolio Reflection Sheet

Name: _____ Date: _____ Assignment: _____

1. What aspect of this work are you most proud of? How is it superior to your previous work? (Explain with as much detail as possible.)

2. What aspects of this work were you disappointed with? (Explain with as much detail as possible.)

3. What will do you differently on your next assignment to improve the quality of your work? (Explain with as much detail as possible.)

their hearts that they are good at their jobs and can prevail regardless of the obstacles. The only proven way to build that belief system is with credible evidence of continuous progress.

When we, in our role as academic coaches, assist our knowledge workers in setting meaningful goals and help them to track their own progress, we create a feedback loop that builds powerful feelings of competence. With each item added to their portfolio of personal bests, students have one more reason to believe in themselves.

It is not just students who need credible feedback. If teachers continue to work in a data vacuum, if the only evidence provided of their value is the often erroneous conclusion drawn from a supervisor's two observations, it will be hard for them to feel like true professionals. However, in this era of high stakes and high standards, if we collect data one student at a time and look at how well our students are developing and how fast they are moving, then we can legitimately rejoice in the success produced through our coaching. Earlier I asked why someone would coach track in Oregon. I could also ask, "Why would someone teach in this high-stress era of high-stakes accountability?"

The answer to both questions is the same. Teachers continue to teach because they care about their students and believe that their students deserve the best possible education. When teachers have the evidence that they are, in fact, providing students with an excellent education, the incessant rain and all the hassles of the workplace just don't seem that bad.

Chapter 3

Strengthening Our Sense of Belonging

O ur behavior on the weekends and during vacation provides a window into the nature of the environments where we feel comfortable. Perhaps the most significant feature about spending time away from work is that we are free to choose where to go, what to do, and whom we want to be with. Although these decisions aren't exclusively left to us, it is a rare occasion when our opinions aren't solicited and our viewpoints considered. Generally, regardless of the final decision, it is important to feel that someone heard our thoughts and we felt included in the decision. Why? If we feel that we weren't consulted, we may decide to opt out. Children seldom have the option of not going along with a decision, consequently they do not feel involved and they misbehave and make everyone else miserable.

In short, when we have good reason to believe that others value our opinions and hear our voice, we feel that we belong. Of course, the feeling of belonging is not the only factor that contributes to or hinders the likelihood that we feel wanted.

The very act of invitation conveys a powerful message about how people regard others. Invitation, like many important words, has more than one meaning. On the most concrete level, it means a request to participate as, for example, when we invite others to a party or other exclusive event. But, invitations are not always formal. When we are invited in the sense of being included in a social group, we intuitively understand that we are wanted by the way group members behave toward us. Those messages are every bit as clear as the words on a printed invitation.

Making School Invitational to All

Each summer every child receives a written invitation to attend school. Starting dates are announced in the newspaper, and flyers are sent to each home. Even a daily schedule is prepared in advance of the student's arrival. Each teacher is assigned a mailbox, a room, and a schedule. Do those facts alone convey the message that the student or teacher is valued or wanted? Most would say no. Feeling invited implies much more than just having a seat assignment. Bill Purkey and his colleagues (Stanley & Purkey, 1994; Purkey & Strahan, 1995; Purkey & Novak, 1996; Cloer & Alexander, 1992) wrote extensively about the need to make education invitational. Invitational education is about the search for ways to make it clear to students that they are truly valued as members of their class and student body. In a study on the effectiveness of schools serving at-risk students, Wehlage and colleagues observed the following:

> They want to belong and to be accepted as part of a peer group, but they also want the support and approval of adults. In our interviews with students, we repeatedly encountered expressions reflecting the importance of membership in the school. Asked about the strengths of their alternative school, students persistently described ways in which these were friendlier and more caring places than their previous schools had been. They talked about peers accepting them and teachers caring about them. They volunteered their observations about the importance of adults displaying a willingness to help them overcome academic and personal problems, and the value of being accepted as an individual (Wehlage, 1989, p. 114).

But the need or desire to feel cared for is not only a concern of youth. Every school district collective bargaining agreement that I've reviewed contains a clause regarding the right to voluntary transfer. Why is this? You can be sure management didn't insert those provisions. The reason the employees demand this right is because teachers, like everyone else, find it unacceptable to be trapped in an environment in which they feel out of place or uncomfortable. As young adults, we transferred from colleges where we felt we didn't fit; some of us left jobs where we didn't feel appreciated; some of us have even dissolved marriage partnerships that failed to meet our needs. Adults who feel out of place regularly exercise the option to leave. But what options exist for students?

The older students can drop out, and many do. Recent drop-out figures (Greene, 2002) show that nearly one out of four high school students leaves school prior to graduation. For African American and Latino students, the figure is closer to one out of two. This isn't just a problem for teenagers. Younger students also drop out. Although they may be unable to leave the school building, many are simply absent socially, intellectually, and emotionally. To help thwart this isolation or alienation, we will examine several successful strategies for helping students and teachers experience a true sense of connection in their work environments.

The Concept of the Inclusive Classroom

Few reform concepts hold more promise, yet are more misunderstood, than the concept of inclusion. In response to powerful research documenting that students with disabilities experience greater success in mainstream classrooms, the Education of All Handicapped Children Act, Public Law 94-142 (1975) mandated that students with identified disabilities be educated in the "least restrictive environment." What this meant for teachers was that children who had heretofore been excluded from their classrooms were now side-by-side with regular education students. Meanwhile, the special education department retained control over the education of these children, and special education staff frequently sat beside them in a separate corner of the room and unobtrusively provided specialized services. Although these mainstreamed students did better than their counterparts in traditional special education classes, a student sitting alone and working on different material is not a fully included member of the class.

Similarly, when school desegregation was outlawed by the 14th Amendment, black students, who began attending the same schools and participating in the same classes as white students, didn't necessarily experience warm feelings of belonging. In reality, the norm in many desegregated schools was that two separate communities forged a truce and lived separate lives side-by-side. In the cafeteria, blacks ate with blacks, and whites ate with whites. The races segregated themselves in the stands at athletic events, on dates, and in most school social activities. Similarly, although mainstreaming may have ended the denial of services and facilities to previously excluded students, it did not confer the benefits or the feelings of full citizenship necessary for these students to truly feel welcome.

When educators recognized that even mainstream students were being "excluded," the concept of *inclusive education* came to the forefront and revised federal regulations for special education stipulated inclusion. Essentially, inclusion meant it would no longer be enough to simply grant equal access to those who had been excluded. It was now expected that they be included as full, valued members of the classroom and school community.

The concept of inclusive education has been a radical notion. Although the term slides easily off the tongue, it is much easier said than done. Inclusion challenges nearly every organizational concept of the modern school. Modern school systems are built on the expectation of homogeneity. We organize schools by grade levels. We support this organizational structure with curricula that have scope and sequence that presume, for example, that all 3rd graders are ready for 3rd grade work and at the end of 3rd grade they will be equipped to do whatever is expected of a 4th grader. We expect the 3rd grade teacher to have mastered the teaching required by the 3rd grade program, but there is no expectation that the teacher will be able to teach students who are ready for upper-grade work or still need help with 1st grade objectives. Furthermore, if time needs to be spent working with students who aren't yet ready for 3rd grade work, it is usually perceived as an unwarranted distraction from the job we were hired to do.

In the last decade, many schools simply declared that they were becoming inclusive. Teachers left a school with conventional expectations in June and returned to an inclusive organization in September. Although the students in their classes were more diverse, the system in which the teacher worked hadn't changed. Teachers were still being told that they were responsible for delivering a specific grade-level curriculum, but now they were also told to meaningfully include students who might not have the requisite readiness or perhaps were so advanced that grade-level work simply wasn't appropriate. Is it any wonder that teachers presented with this changed expectation, but with no training or support, felt frustrated and poorly equipped to do the job? Is it any wonder that many of the most advanced children continue to feel bored and that students who enter the classroom lacking in skills continue to feel inadequate?

The problem is not that inclusion isn't a good idea. Rather what wasn't understood is that it is a big system idea, not a minor instructional adjustment. Inclusion requires an almost complete reconsideration of the way educators have organized and conducted education for the past century. Most significantly, meaningful inclusion requires changes in how we make decisions, how we teach, and how we work with our colleagues.

How Are Classroom Decisions Made?

In the mythical world of the truly homogeneous classroom, democratic decision making isn't a pressing issue. Because all children gather in the same place at the same time, their teachers, as philosopher kings, are in an appropriate position to determine and implement their view of what the students (as a group) in the class need. But, how does a teacher address the modern classroom—a place where students from different cultures, families, backgrounds, skill sets, and educational needs are thrust together and called a class? Today's teachers must supervise a collection of unique and autonomous individuals, not a classroom community where each student will automatically give allegiance. For many of us, this is an untenable battle. Few teachers are capable of simultaneously negotiating and following through on agreements made with the 30 or more idiosyncratic individuals typically found in an elementary classroom or the 150-plus students in secondary schools.

Democratic Classrooms and School Governance

If teachers weren't supportive of democratic classroom governance for moral and ethical reasons, it is now imperative if we are to achieve success with inclusive classrooms. What do we mean by democratic classroom governance? Does it mean an abdication of responsibility by the teacher? Does it mean that students are free to ignore school, district, or state mandates?

No. As citizens in a democracy, we recognize that many times laws and policies won't be to our liking, but that does not empower us to act as though they didn't exist. Students need to understand this. They need also to understand the rationale for a citizen's willingness to follow expectations (even ones they do not like) in democratic societies. What makes acquiescing to society's expectations tenable in a democracy is that we know we are fully empowered participants in the process of developing and implementing the laws and policies. In short, in a democracy the citizens know that their voices are heard and their votes counted even if their side lacks the support to prevail.

Consider how you would feel if you were living in a totalitarian state where both the direction of policy and the rules and regulations that govern daily life ran counter to your desires and beliefs. How would this make you feel? Would this be a situation in which you would want to invest your best effort? Or would you be more likely to put forth no more than the minimum? This is the circumstance in which too many students and too many teachers find themselves. The first and best place to begin addressing this problem is through changes to the classroom and school governance processes.

The Concept of the Democratic Classroom

The concept of the democratic classroom is not without controversy. Some argue that children aren't experienced enough to know what they need and how they should behave. This is precisely why society empowers adults to take responsibility for the education of minors. Conversely, others argue that children's desires should compose the very core of their education.

Fortunately, democracy isn't an all-or-nothing concept. Classrooms and schools, like all civil societies, can be democratic by degree. It is critical that teachers feel comfortable, whatever way their classrooms are organized and operated. To ask teachers to incorporate a model that is antithetical to their belief system not only contributes to teacher stress, but also provides little or no benefit to students. Our students need for us to be authentic. Implementing strategies we neither agree with nor are comfortable using leaves us looking dishonest and ultimately undermines our effectiveness.

Involving Students in Instructional Decision Making

The first question you'll want to ponder when planning for student involvement in instruction is "Why are teachers here?" The creation of schools was not a random act. Communities don't tax themselves and regulate their children's lives on a whim. The community expects educators to accomplish some specific things.

After spending some time considering our purpose as teachers, it is wise to compare and validate our perceptions with the views of colleagues. An open discussion on the role and purpose of the teacher is an excellent agenda item for a faculty, department, or grade-level meeting. It can also be an important topic for a parent forum. Once you are comfortable with your answer to that fundamental question, it is time to move to the next step, soliciting the student voice.

Soliciting the Student Voice and Setting Boundaries

It is in soliciting the student voice that you, the teacher, need to engage in some deep soul searching. You need to determine the areas in which you will invite student involvement and which areas are out of bounds. It is always a bad idea to solicit student input if it won't or cannot be seriously considered. On the other hand, when students are sincerely asked to present their ideas with the knowledge that the community will consider those ideas, it is a personally affirming experience.

At one time, it was widely felt that when in school, students were to obey their elders without question. Consequently, all the decisions pertaining to children's education were made by the adults for the children. Nowadays, some teachers believe the complete opposite: that everything in education ought to be determined and directed by the students themselves. Some educators even argue that the very goals and expected outcomes of schooling should be governed by student choice. Although there may be some value in that perspective, most public school teachers will find themselves uncomfortable with that extreme position, especially in this era of standards. Whether we like it or not, in most jurisdictions students and schools must demonstrate proficiency and growth on specific objectives. Ignoring these objectives or failing to give them their due places us, our schools, and, most important, our students in peril.

Separating the ends from the means

We can resolve this by dividing classroom work that is done by the teacher and by students into two separate categories, the ends and the means.

In this era of standards, I would honestly tell my students that the overwhelming majority of the ends (if not all) have already been set for us. Although we may like them or hate them, we cannot ignore them because promotion, graduation, tenure, and so forth are based upon our success in meeting them.

The means used to arrive at those ends are rarely stipulated by policy. Thus teacher creativity, empowerment, and discretion become important in determining the means. Each teacher possesses a degree of freedom in regard to the means they employ. We can, quite legitimately, based upon our expertise, make unilateral decisions on how we deliver instruction in our classroom. If we want, we can assume full responsibility for inspiring and helping our students acquire all the expected knowledge and skills. Or, we can elect to share some of this decision making with the students. That decision is up to us.

The way I resolve questions about student involvement in instructional decision making is by reflecting on three questions about each goal or objective:

1. Do I believe there is only one way to accomplish this?
2. Do I believe there is a best way to accomplish this?
3. Do I believe there are multiple ways to accomplish this objective?

If I answer Question 1 with an emphatic yes, then the only ethical course is to implement that particular strategy. I explain to my students the rationale for choosing this strategy, and I am comfortable telling them that based upon research and my professional judgment, this is the approach I determined we must follow. Although this won't guarantee that my students will love the strategy, it will ensure that they at least understand my rationale for doing it this way.

When the answer to Question 1 is no and my answer to Question 2 is yes, then I use this approach: I tell the students about the strategy that I, personally and professionally, believe will work best. However, I also tell them that though I see a great deal to commend this approach, I am aware that it is not the only strategy that could get us to our desired destination.

After I have acknowledged that there are multiple ways to get to our outcome, I ask the students if they can think of alternative approaches that should be considered. When using this strategy, I don't feel obligated to remain passive. In fact, I feel we do our students a disservice when we don't share our opinions and explain why we favor one approach over another.

After engaging the students in a dialogue, occasionally they will coalesce around an approach that I am not comfortable using. In those cases, I will reluctantly exercise my authority and implement another strategy that I believe is in their best interest. When I feel I must overrule student sentiment, I try to emphasize three things:

1. I understood their position;
2. I seriously considered their ideas; however,
3. I decided on this course of action based on a sincere concern regarding what I believe to be their best interest.

Usually I feel that the approach favored by the students has a good likelihood of succeeding (i.e., in getting them to mastery with the desired objective), in which case I go with the students' proposal.

The process described in Implementation Strategy 3.1 will help you decide on the degree of student involvement that fits best with your values and beliefs about teaching and learning.

Implementation Strategy 3.1

Giving Students a Voice in Instruction

Step 1. Define the Purpose

Spend some time reflecting on the question, "Why do we require students to attend school?"

After you've collected your thoughts, it is helpful to write them in bulleted form. Your list may contain items such as the following:

- To help students acquire the skills necessary for lifelong learning,
- To help students develop curiosity and wonder regarding their world,
- To help students develop strength of character, and
- To help students acquire mastery of key facts, concepts, and skills.

Step 2. Set Boundaries and Solicit the Student Voice

Begin by asking yourself which of the purposes that surfaced (in Step 1) do you feel comfortable having influenced by student opinion? Do this by asking three questions of each educational purpose you identified:

1. Do I believe there is only one way to accomplish this?
2. Do I believe there is a best way to accomplish this?
3. Do I believe there are multiple ways to accomplish this objective?

If you answered Question 1 with a yes, then you have an ethical responsibility to use the appropriate strategy. Inform the students that based upon research and your professional judgment, this is the approach we will follow.

If, however, you answered Question 1 with a no, and Question 2 with a yes, then you might want to follow another strategy. Explain to the students why you favor a particular strategy. Tell them you are willing to consider their ideas but will incorporate their ideas only if they can make a persuasive argument for doing so. If they succeed in presenting a sound rationale, you may want to use some of their ideas.

If after listening to student suggestions you still hold serious reservations about the approach they favor, you should implement the strategy you believe best. When finding it necessary to reject student proposals, you should be sure they know that

1. You understood their position;
2. You seriously considered their ideas; and
3. Your decision was based upon a sincere commitment to what you believed was in their best interest.

If you answered questions 1 and 2 with a no, then tell the students that there are several ways to accomplish the objective. Provide them with some alternatives and ask for suggestions. Then encourage them to develop logical and sound arguments as to why one of your alternatives or one of their own invention should be employed.

Step 3. Make a Decision

After class discussion of the arguments, pro and con, of the alternative strategies, make a community decision on the strategy to be used.

There are several reasons to use the approach outlined in Implementation Strategy 3.1, even in circumstances when you might believe another strategy is better. You may be asking, "Why would a dedicated professional go along with a strategy that he might not think is best?" Here are the reasons I will go along with a student suggestion, even when I don't necessarily believe it to be the best idea:

1. My students will have a vested interest in making their strategy succeed. After all, the strategy would never have been employed were it not for their advocacy of it.

2. I will be triggering a Hawthorne Effect, which refers to the tendency of subjects in experimental situations to improve their performance as an artifact of the experimental situation. My students will be engaged in an experiment to prove that their hypothesis (i.e., how to best accomplish this objective) is correct. The desire to prove the worthiness of their hypothesis will inevitably inspire more commitment and effort than would be generated were they following an imposed approach.

3. The youthful need to challenge authority is thwarted. The only reason the students are learning the material this way is because they believe in it. They have become the authority.

4. It is a way that I can encourage a sense of ownership or membership in the class. Having the teacher follow a strategy that the class members have advocated powerfully demonstrates my conviction that this is their class, and they have a voice in its direction.

Teaching Democracy

I have often lamented the sorry state of social studies in U.S. schools. I love the U.S. system of governance that generations of citizens have built upon the vision of Jefferson, Madison, and our nation's other founders. Although certainly not yet perfect, I believe it is the best model of democracy ever produced. What has grieved me, however, is that as teachers, we haven't been more successful in exciting our students about this unique accomplishment. I suspect the reason for this is that though we preach democracy, we give children little opportunity to experience it in action.

One way to bring democracy to life is by engaging students in each of four key facets of democratic living:

1. Creating a just framework (i.e., a Constitution),
2. Establishing necessary and fair rules and regulations (i.e., laws),
3. Assessing performance (i.e., openly discussing data and assembling the facts), and
4. Adjusting future policy based on data (i.e., making informed democratic decisions).

A Class Constitution

Several years ago when I was the head teacher at an alternative school for high school dropouts, I stumbled upon a powerful teaching strategy. At the time, I was responsible for teaching a group of alienated and remedial students the required U.S. history course. They did not approach this curriculum with any enthusiasm, and they truly believed that the subject had no relevance to their lives. A few weeks into the term, I faced the daunting task of teaching the Constitution. To say the least, my students could not have been less interested.

Reaching for a way to make this study of a 200-year-old document meaningful, I contrasted for the students the situation that the 13 newly created states found themselves in with the situation facing our own radical and new school. Without thinking through where this was all going, I prepared a two-column worksheet. In one column, I typed each article of the U.S. Constitution; the other column was left blank. I asked the students to see if they could craft a parallel Constitution for our school. I wish that I could take credit for being smart enough to predict what was about to happen. They were able to see a parallel for nearly every article and wanted to include those concepts in our constitution. They even started believing that the founding fathers were one group of "cool dudes"!

For example, the students recognized the need for foreign relations (i.e., analogous to communications and negotiations with the other schools in the district); the need for congressional (i.e., community) approval of the budget; and the necessity for separate executive, legislative, and judicial branches. I was truly unprepared for the enthusiasm this engendered. I soon realized I had unleashed a movement I had not anticipated. The students weren't willing to see this as a purely academic exercise. They wanted to ratify and be governed by their own constitution. What quickened my pulse was seeing all the power they vested in the executive, which being parallel to our national government was an elected position. Would the school district, which was bound by board policy, union contracts, as well as state and federal law, allow a former dropout to exercise powers generally carried out only by a principal? But, alas, I underestimated my students. Realizing that the community of nations (i.e., the district) would have trouble negotiating with or accepting the legitimacy of a student in this position, they elected me to be their president.

Once I was sworn in, I breathed a sigh of relief. Not only was I confident that, in the exercise of my power, I wouldn't raise the hackles of the superintendent, I also didn't fear the impeachment clause. After all, I always felt that if the kids wanted me out, the only smart thing for me to do was to make a graceful exit.

Space won't permit me to share everything that transpired, but suffice it to say that in no time these students had a deeper understanding of the issues faced by the early states than many advanced-placement students. More important, as we followed our constitution, the students demonstrated a degree of ownership and responsibility for the school that I haven't seen since. I clearly recall one hotly contested case when the supreme court found me liable for a misuse of school funds—I hadn't sought prior congressional approval for a field trip.

I don't expect, nor would I advise, other teachers to replicate this process. A grievance filed by the teachers' union when the students attempted to impeach my successor is reason enough to avoid this strategy. However, the lessons I learned from this experience are well worth remembering.

The former dropouts attending the alternative school were a group of teenagers that most people in our community felt were incapable of accepting and demonstrating responsibility. They were wrong. The act of participation in the development of a framework for democratic governance was all it took to build feelings of legitimacy for our social contract. The students protected our constitutional way of life. For them, the rule of law as embodied by our constitution was sacred.

Perhaps even more surprising was the seriousness with which they approached the governance process. Most of us would be happy if our legislators reflected upon policy as deeply as these teenagers did. Remember, it was the students who determined that the school would be better served with an adult school employee as president.

Creating a Class Constitution

Determine the givens

Before introducing the concept of democratic governance, consider which things are, or should be, nonnegotiable. For me this always begins with school rules. For example, my students must regularly attend class, refrain from being tardy, and take all required state and district exams. Although my students might not support these expectations, they generally appreciate my directness regarding that which is legitimately under their control and that which ultimately lies outside their sphere of influence.

Beyond school rules, you will likely bring to the surface other expectations that must be in place for you to be comfortable as the teacher or academic coach. For instance, I have always insisted that any behavior and language that undermines the dignity of any person or group is unacceptable in our classroom.

Encourage compliance

The greatest value of having the students establish classroom bylaws is that it forges deeper ownership of the classroom community's shared goals. It would be ideal in any community if all the laws and regulations were followed consistently by every citizen. But, just as this doesn't occur in the larger society, it is unlikely to be the case in your classroom. Therefore, you will need to engage the students in consideration of what the classroom community should do to maximize compliance through a set of bylaws.

When bringing up the issue of compliance, I find students will initially focus on enforcement and punishment. When this occurs, I suggest, "Let's not get sidetracked into deciding what to do in cases of violations, instead let's consider what can be done to encourage class members to voluntarily follow their own rules."

Make changes as necessary

No one is able to predict the future with precision. Things change, new needs arise, and rules and regulations often have unintended consequences. Even with the greatness of the U.S. Constitution, the citizens have felt it necessary to modify it more than 20 times. For this reason, when designing a class constitution it is important to consider in advance how adjustments will be made if circumstances call for change.

When I ask my students, "What do you think is an appropriate process for the consideration of adjustments?" I use the U.S. Constitution as an example. I share with them the belief of the framers that it ought to be hard to overturn a democratically made decision. Furthermore, I tell them that it is our obligation as citizens to do everything possible to make our laws work as intended. However, if after giving a rule or process an honest chance to succeed, it becomes evident to the community that adjustments are needed, there should be a way to have this accomplished.

As I said earlier, it isn't necessary to invest the time required to produce as elaborate a document as my alternative school students did. Unless your job is awfully secure, it might even be deemed unwise. However, the essential elements of this process can be used in any classroom and will provide significant motivational benefits. Implementation Strategy 3.2 will help take you and your students through the process of designing a class constitution.

Implementation Strategy 3.2

Creating a Class Constitution

Step 1. Prepare a List of Givens

Consider what school rules and teacher expectations are nonnegotiable. Share this list with your students, explaining why these are not open to debate.

Step 2. Solicit Ideas on Social Needs

Engage your students in a discussion of what issues everyone needs to address if the classroom is to be a productive place for learning and student development. Collect these and place them on a poster or on the board in front of the room.

Step 3. Develop Equitable Processes

In small groups, have the students review each social need on the list and discuss how the classroom community might best organize itself to accommodate that need. Have each group report its findings and then as a class decide which process or combination of processes will work best for this classroom community.

Step 4. Decide on Procedures or Bylaws

In small groups, ask the students to consider what procedures will work best to help this community stay true to its commitments. Groups then share what they came up with and the class selects or combines the ideas into an agreed-upon set of bylaws.

Step 5. Decide on an Assessment Process

Point out to your students the fact that democracy is a constantly evolving experiment. As a class, discuss what types of data or information are needed to determine whether the classroom bylaws and procedures are, in fact, accomplishing their objective. Agree to a time frame for collecting that data and reviewing the bylaws and procedures.

Step 6. Create an Amendment Process

Raise the question, "What should we do if our data tell us that our rules and procedures aren't accomplishing the intended purpose?" Have students deliberate and decide upon a process for adjusting or amending the bylaws as necessary.

Spending a year living under a class constitution of their own making, and making adjustments when both the evidence and the membership deem it necessary, will go a long way toward helping students feel that they belong in your class.

School as Institution or School as Family

Knowing that your community values your ideas, beliefs, and opinions provides you with powerful evidence that you belong. Nevertheless, a deep sense of affiliation requires more than simply being listened to or being empowered to make decisions. Our homes, the places where most of us feel most comfortable, are filled with physical and emotional mementos. It is impossible to confuse your house with anyone else's home. You see your footprints everywhere. You see yourself reflected in the décor, in the feel of the house, even in the projects that you have yet to complete. Seeing yourself in the surroundings confirms that this is your place. This sense of being home comes as much from the feel of an environment as it does from its physical attributes.

A window into this phenomenon can be found in the language teachers use to describe our workplace. Do I refer to the school where I work as "my" school or do I call it "the" school? I was first alerted to this phenomenon by listening to the directors of extracurricular activities at the school where I was principal. It was more than their words. When I heard a coach referring to "my team" or a director talking about "her choir," it conveyed more than possessiveness; it implied all that is good about a proprietary relationship. Nearly all teachers refer to the place where they teach as "my classroom," but they don't necessarily refer to the campus as "my school." What does this tell us? When we are absent from our place, we are missed. This is because we belong there. But, our presence at an impersonal place, such as a stadium or a shopping center, is merely a statistic.

As schools became larger and more complex during the 20th century, both educators and the larger society began to see schools as organizations or institutions. This perception was not meant to convey that schools were inhuman, but that they had a life and purpose that transcended the particular people who worked in them. Administrators, who were no longer principal-teachers, were hired to manage or lead these complex organizations, and the instructional personnel who worked in the schools began to be seen as interchangeable parts. For example, many school districts now have policies that mandate moving administrators on a regular basis, arguing that they get stale if they stay in the same place for too long.

Let's contrast the school environment with another environment where people spend much of their most treasured time—the family. No one would disagree that the family is an important and influential environment. Everyone wants families to be vital and functional. So, would anyone seriously say it is important for children to change mothers every five years, so that the kids don't get into a rut? I always cringe a little when I hear it said that, due to a retirement, a transfer, or resignation, a teacher needs to be replaced. The word *replaced* implies that the members of the school family are interchangeable parts. Imagine saying to a child, "Your brother has gone to college, so we need to replace him."

None of this is to say that families don't change. They do all the time. Children move away, loved ones die, and, unfortunately, divorce happens. But when these events occur, a mark is left. People notice that a special part of the fabric of their lives has changed.

When people play a role in the life of a community and they leave, they are missed. Although the football coach may realize that people will miss him if he retires or takes another job, how often do sophomore English teachers feel the same way about their role at school?

If membership on the staff is to convey a true sense of belonging, then faculty members need to play meaningful roles outside the isolated and private confines of their classroom. Earlier I spoke of the importance of a class constitution to build a sense of ownership for students. It is equally important to make sure that the manner in which the adult school community takes care of its collective business conveys a sense of ownership and importance for the faculty.

Meaningful School Governance

In recent years, it has become the vogue to move toward more participatory governance in schools. Teachers sit on site councils and advisory committees. Faculty representatives are on nearly every committee that deals with school issues. Unfortunately, though, more often than not, this type of participation ends up being just another form of political correctness or window dressing. Teachers spend valuable time at meetings yet don't feel empowered because many of the most common forms of teacher involvement, like many forms of parent involvement, don't take into account the needs, skills, and potential contributions of the participants.

Like most busy people, I have no desire to participate in each and every decision that happens around me. In fact, I appreciate it when other capable people see to it that many of the things I need are taken care of for me. That being said, it is also very important to me that with certain issues, the ones that pertain to my top priorities, I have a meaningful say.

Determining which decisions call for whose input is best worked out in a shared governance plan.

The Process of Collegial School Governance

The work agenda

All people should have an opportunity to contribute their insights to the school's work agenda, by which I mean those items that must be attended to in order for the school to effectively and efficiently meet its educational goals. In September, when reflecting on what needs to be done, a faculty could conclude that they will need to

- Adopt new science texts,
- Develop a schedule for the 7th and 8th grade teams,
- Study the adoption of a flexible block schedule,
- Complete fund raising for the new weight room,
- Align curriculum with the new state standards,
- Redesign or redecorate the faculty room,
- Increase attendance at parent advisory meetings,
- Fine-tune the teacher advisory program,
- Implement an intramural program, and
- Review the talented and gifted program.

Categorizing the work agenda

Once the professional staff has taken stock of the work ahead, it becomes obvious that the work covers the entire waterfront. The tasks range from adopting instructional materials to interior decorating. To make sense of this diverse scope of work, organize the tasks by category. The proposed work could be categorized in the following way:

- Building environment issues—faculty room redecorating,
- Program specific issues—science texts, weight-room funding,
- Scheduling decisions—block schedule,
- Community relations—parent advisory meetings,
- Compliance issues—alignment to state standards,
- Schoolwide noncurricular programs—intramural program, and
- Schoolwide programs—teacher advisory program.

Continuum of involvement

Democratic decisions can be made in a number of ways. Sometimes citizens vote for representatives who make decisions on their behalf as is the case with the U.S. Congress, the city council, and the school board. As individual citizens, our input is made when we select someone to represent our interests. For other matters, we ask our elected representatives to select a qualified person to make decisions and then take action on behalf of the community. For example, the president or the governor appoints judges, the school board appoints a superintendent, or the city council hires a director of parks and recreation. However, there are certain issues where people aren't willing to delegate the decision making. When people don't want anyone speaking for them, direct democracy in the form of a referendum or a community vote can occur—for example, a vote on the school budget or a ballot initiative.

Each of these approaches is a democratic process, but they differ in what is expected from the individual citizen. Each fits an empowered citizenry, but each demands a different level

---

Figure 3.1
Sample Decision-Making Structure for a School

Issue or Topic	Decisions made by
Community relations	Administration
Event scheduling	Administration, after requesting and evaluating faculty input
Schoolwide (noncurricular) programs	Administration, after faculty meeting discussion
Building environment	Ad hoc faculty committee
Text adoptions	Grade level or department faculty
Program-specific issues	Grade level or department faculty
Scheduling decisions	Elected faculty senate or council
Compliance with mandated requirements	Consider input from entire faculty
Cross-departmental programs	Entire faculty

---

of commitment, involvement, and accountability. Figure 3.1 demonstrates the range of processes that might be employed by a faculty when dealing with different categories of school decisions.

Reporting decisions

Whatever our level of involvement in decision making, we all want to know about the decisions that affect us. Notification is both a courtesy and a necessity if we are to work effectively as a community. In families, decisions are shared at the dinner table, at a family meeting, or in a note taped to the refrigerator. More often than not, at school they are shared in daily or weekly staff bulletins or reported at faculty meetings. Whatever method is used, it is crucial that all members of a community know where and how they can learn about decisions that affect them.

Process for reconsideration and appeals

Like families, school communities should be flexible and prepared to reconsider decisions when necessary. No one would feel comfortable in a family that refused to consider the unique nature of issues and crises that might emerge from time to time. This is also true for a faculty that wishes to organize itself around a family metaphor.

When developing a collegial participatory governance system, it is good to remember why decisions were delegated in the first place. School communities delegate out of respect for the time pressures and commitments of colleagues. But respect shouldn't end there. Once a decision has been made on the community's behalf, it is important that once again respect be shown for all members of the community. One way respect can be shown is by empowering every community member to call for a reconsideration of a decision. All good governance systems contain a process for the appeal or review of decisions.

When using a continuum of involvement for decision making, appeals are handled by reconsideration or rehearing at the next level of the hierarchy. For example, if an administrative decision on the scheduling of an open house is viewed by a teacher as problematic, that teacher could ask to have it discussed at the next faculty meeting. Or, if the faculty senate decided to change the daily schedule and some staff members felt that this would have an adverse effect on instruction, it could be referred to the entire faculty after departmental deliberations. The following six steps provide an example of an appeals process in a participatory governance system:

1. School decisions will be assigned by category to the levels indicated on our decision-making continuum.

2. Decisions will be reported in the weekly faculty newsletter and in posted meeting minutes, as appropriate.

3. A request for reconsideration must be made within one week of the announcement of the decision.

4. Any member of the faculty can call for reconsideration of a decision that she feels was unwise or might have been improved with more input.

5. When reconsideration is called for, it will be automatically referred to the next highest level on the participation continuum.

6. Steps 1–5 may be repeated—except in emergency situations—until no more requests for reconsideration are received.

Implementation Strategy 3.3 will assist you in the development of an effective and efficient collegial school governance process.

Implementation Strategy 3.3

Developing a Viable School Governance Plan

Step 1. Decide What Needs to Be Done

Call a faculty meeting at the beginning of the school year to set the year's agenda (a school to-do list). Categorize the list by the nature of the items.

Step 2. Agree to a Continuum of Involvement

As a group, brainstorm an array of processes that could be used to make decisions. List and number the processes in descending order of involvement.

Step 3. Assign Responsibility for Each Category of Decision

For each category (Step 1) every faculty member should assign the degree of involvement (Step 2) they feel is appropriate. Compile the responses and discuss the results.

Step 4. Create a Tentative Decision-Making Structure

Based upon the discussion of involvement (Step 3), prepare a proposal reflecting the involvement of stakeholders desired for each category. See Figure 3.1 (p. 62) for an example of a decision-making structure.

Step 5. Ratify the Structure

The entire faculty needs to meet and discuss the proposed decision-making structure. Three questions should frame the discussion:

1. Are we comfortable with the level of involvement assigned to each category of decision?

2. Do we feel that our voices, opinions, and perspectives will be heard on the issues that are important to us?

3. Is the time required to implement this plan reasonable considering our other needs and responsibilities?

Once people reach consensus in answer to those questions, the plan is considered ratified and becomes the community's process for participatory governance.

Step 6. Determine the Appeals Process

A last step prior to implementation is designing an appeal process. Deliberate the answers to two questions:

1. Who should be empowered to request an appeal of a decision made through the governance process?
2. How will appeals be handled? (see pp. 62–63)

The strategy for developing a school governance plan ensures that everyone's opinion is heard and is considered on those issues that matter most to him; yet no one is required to invest time on issues that could just as well be dealt with by others. Such a process goes a long way toward having the workings of the school carry the imprint of the faculty and making the school a place where teachers feel they belong.

Sense-of-Community Decision Making

Sometimes the assumption is made that the only form of democratic decision making is majority rule. Alternatively, many school leaders now argue that the best way for a faculty to bind itself as a community is by reaching a consensus on every issue. Although on occasion there is merit to both these strategies, other times they produce unwise results and put faculty collegiality and motivation at risk. This is no doubt clear to any teacher who holds positions that are shared by as much as 40 percent of the faculty, yet never get implemented. Having proposals that are widely accepted but never implemented because a slim majority opposes them can be frustrating for any professional. Likewise, any educator who has ever felt the need to trade away deeply held convictions to avoid being branded as an obstacle to consensus can relate to the bad taste consensus can leave in one's mouth.

However, a third alternative—one that builds collegiality, community, and motivation—exists. I call this approach *sense-of-community decision making*. Some readers may have encountered a similar system of decision making called *fist to five*. These two approaches to decision making are built upon three core values:

1. Every member of the faculty possesses wisdom;
2. Every member of the faculty is a fully empowered member of the school community; and, consequently

3. The school community is obligated to take into account the opinions and values of each member.

Whenever a critical issue surfaces, open ongoing discussions are encouraged. Because everyone on the faculty possesses wisdom, full participation is encouraged and discussions are allowed to continue until everyone has had a chance to contribute. To end a discussion prematurely could result in the failure to consider a valuable insight or perspective.

Once all members have had time to talk and the group seems to be coalescing around a position, the convener summarizes what is understood to be the prevailing sentiment. I will use a faculty deliberation over a reading adoption to illustrate how the process works.

Noticing what appears to be general agreement among the faculty, the convener summarizes the group's viewpoint as follows:

> It appears that the faculty favors the approach to reading instruction employed by the Sagor Reading Series and therefore feels that this is the program we should adopt.

Now it is time for the community to either affirm the convener's understanding of group sentiment or correct it. This is accomplished by calling for a sense of community.

Generally, a sense of community is called immediately after the deliberation, while everyone is still present. If the group is too large or geographically dispersed, a sense of community can also be taken in written form. Consistent with the three core beliefs, a set of ground rules must accompany the sense-of-community process. The following ground rules are examples:

1. All members of the community have an obligation to share their opinion; therefore, abstaining and preserving the right to criticize a community decision is not an option;

2. The community has an obligation to consider and work to incorporate the ideas of dissenters in the formulation of a final decision; and

3. No decision will be implemented if it violates the moral or deeply held beliefs of any member of the community.

When the convener calls for a sense of community, every member of the group must respond in one of the following ways:

■ If community members find themselves whole-heartedly agreeing with the statement of the convener, they raise one finger or write down the number (1).

■ If members find themselves in fundamental agreement with the sentiment expressed by the convener, they raise two fingers or write down a number (2).

■ If members are torn—they see merits and concur with most of the proposal, yet still hold concerns—they raise three fingers or write a (3).

■ If members don't like the proposal, find it is not what they would recommend, but are willing to go along; they raise four fingers or award it a score of (4).

■ If, however, any members of the community hold such negative views about the proposal that they cannot support it in good conscience, they raise a fist or award a five (5), and the proposal (as was stated by the convener) is effectively vetoed!

The process then continues. In sense-of-community decision making, the power of veto is extended to everyone because of the first core value. As every member of the group is presumed to possess wisdom, then there must be good reason whenever a veto is made. It means a valued member of the group has seen something the rest of group missed or is sensitive to something that might have been overlooked.

This is when the ground rules come into play. Ground Rule 1 requires all members to share their opinion. Therefore, the dissenter is asked to present the rationale for the veto. Let's assume that Mr. Ricardo, the teacher exercising the veto on the reading adoption, says,

> While I see merit in the Sagor Reading Series, I am very concerned that it could put as much as 20 percent of our students at risk. For students with the requisite readiness, this program is great, but it doesn't make allowances for children who are still having difficulty decoding. I'm afraid that if we use this program, a number of our children may fail with reading and that will jeopardize their entire school career.

Ground Rule 2 obligates the group to work at incorporating everyone's perspective into a final decision. So it is now time for the group to reconsider and modify the proposal in light of the views expressed by Mr. Ricardo. This occurs by the convener asking, "What modifications could now be made to our proposal that would incorporate Mr. Ricardo's concerns?"

The deliberations continue until it again appears that the group is coalescing around a proposal—one that responds to Mr. Ricardo's concern. The convener summarizes the understanding of the revised group sentiment.

> The group feels that the Sagor Reading Series (SRS) should be adopted and used in all of our classrooms because it holds promise for the overwhelming majority of our students. However, we also recognize that there may be some students who are likely to need a more structured, sequential, and phonetically based approach if they are to develop reading proficiency. Therefore, we will make a supplemental adoption of the Tams Reading Program (TRP) and will make sure that each teacher has enough sets of the TRP materials to use with students who appear to need a more structured approach.

Another sense-of-community vote is taken. The cycle continues until a proposal emerges that receives an overwhelming number of 1s and 2s and does not receive any vetoes.

Implementation Strategy 3.4 will guide you through the steps to making a sense-of-community decision.

Implementation Strategy 3.4

Using the Sense-of-Community Process to Make Decisions

Step 1. Calling for a Decision

When the leader or convener of a faculty dialogue believes that the community (faculty) has reached a decision or resolution to a problem, the leader or convener summarizes what is understood to be the sentiment of the group.

At this point, the convener calls for a sense of the community.

Step 2. Taking the Sense of Community

All participants share their position on the proposal by raising their fingers or writing numbers (1–5). Should no veto (5) be exercised, yet there are few 1s and 2s, it probably means the proposal is not widely endorsed and further deliberation should occur.

Step 3. Responding to a Veto

Should any participant exercise a veto (5), the process comes to a standstill. The person exercising the veto is asked to articulate his objection.

Once the group understands the rationale for the veto, additional discussion occurs. The focus is on modifying the proposal in a manner that incorporates the concerns expressed. Discussion continues until a modified proposal has emerged that appears to be acceptable to all.

Step 4. Reaching the Final Decision

The convener reads the modified proposal and another sense of community is taken. If the new proposal receives an overwhelming number of 1s and 2s and isn't vetoed, then a decision has been made and the community can congratulate itself on making a wise and inclusive decision.

Sense-of-community decision making conveys a powerful sense of belonging. When I know that my colleagues care enough about my opinions to allow me to veto a decision, even one embraced by the overwhelming majority, it tells me I am a valued and respected member of the family. Consequently, out of respect for my colleagues, I will be judicious in the exercise of my right to veto.

Internal Consultancy

Collective Autonomy

This term *collective autonomy,* originally coined by Carl Glickman (1993) has profound implications. It may seem like an oxymoron, but the term has great meaning for a school community:

1. If a faculty is to be successful, it must hold a shared, collective vision of success. The first step in hitting a target is to clearly see it. If we are to arrive at a destination together, we need to be crystal clear and in agreement on what constitutes the agreed-upon destination. Such agreement is the *collective* aspect of collective autonomy.

2. With the exception of the rare case when we have proof that one approach will work for everyone in every situation, we are well served to maximize the opportunities for creativity and autonomy in the design and execution of alternative strategies to succeed with our shared objectives. This is the *autonomy* aspect of collective autonomy.

What binds the school community together and conveys the sense that we are members of a family is the knowledge that we are all committed to achieving the same outcomes. Furthermore, by inviting and respecting the exploration of a variety of approaches to achieving success on our outcomes, we express our confidence in the potential of each community member to design what might prove to be an innovative and successful strategy. Nevertheless, the community will want and need data on the efficacy of all alternative approaches that are being implemented to advance our collective vision. Unless or until it is found that one strategy will work with all students better than any other, it is unwise as well as disrespectful to colleagues to arbitrarily restrict creative exploration into what could well be a superior approach.

When teachers experiment with creative strategies to realize shared objectives, they develop expertise and insights that will be of interest and value to the entire school community. Internal consultancy is one way for teachers to share their expertise with each other. Implementation Strategy 3.5 outlines the steps to follow when developing an Internal Consultancy Program at your school and the focus can be broadened to your district.

Implementation Strategy 3.5

Implementing an Internal Consultancy Program

Building capacity for internal consultancy is easy. It is accomplished by following four specific steps:

Step 1. Call for Ideas

At a faculty meeting, all faculty members are encouraged to submit a two- or three-sentence description of a strategy they will be using to address one of the school's priority teaching-learning objectives (e.g., the development of critical thinking, skillful expository writing, or math problem solving).

Step 2. Share Strategies

Faculty members share their descriptions with everyone else (at the meeting, on a faculty room bulletin board, or in a staff newsletter). An example of a set of alternative expository writing strategies follows:

Building on student interest (Emma M.)

I will begin by having my students think through their position on something that needs to be changed at school. Then I will have them write an essay justifying their position, which they will send to the principal. Later we will look at what made certain essays better than others and establish class criteria on quality.

Developing style through modeling (Robert J.)

I am having my students read several essays by well-known writers. As a class, we will then dissect these works to determine what makes them good. Then I will have the kids write essays in the style of each author. Finally, I will have them write their own essays in their own voices.

Integrating literature study (Ellisa T.)

I will be integrating expository writing into our literature study. My students will be required to write reviews of each piece of work that we will later critique as a class.

Step 3. Report on Results

Once data are available on the success obtained or problems encountered, they are shared through a consultancy bulletin. An example of an internal consultancy bulletin about expository writing follows:

Using student interest (Emma M.)

I was surprised by how well the students took to this assignment. In fact, in the course evaluation they said this was their favorite class activity. I knew they liked it, as the fluency of their writing was the best I obtained all term. However, I was really disappointed with the criteria the class came up with. It was so off the mark that I had to replace it with the district's rubric. I had hoped they would come to the same place on their own. Apparently, I was mistaken.

Modeling process (Robert J.)

I was pleased with the end result of the work done by my students after using the modeling process. I was, however, surprised at the time it took to complete this unit. Because of this, I had to cut some two weeks off my creative writing unit. Also, my two weakest students became frustrated and failed to turn in at least half of the assignments.

Integrating writing and literature (Ellisa T.)

This was a powerful learning experience for me. Not only was this the best writing my students produced all year (as measured on the district assessment) but it actually saved class time. I ended up spending one week less than when I taught these as separate units. As a result, I had more time to devote to the speech unit (which I combined with the persuasive essay assignment).

Step 4. Access Consulting Assistance

When a faculty member or a faculty work group wants help on a priority objective, they are encouraged to contact colleagues with experience developing successful approaches to attaining that objective.

Certainly, using external consultants is acceptable. But nothing underscores our value to our own communities more than being asked to share our expertise or to help fellow teachers solve problems.

Returning to Inclusion

Earlier in this chapter, I talked about inclusion and the use of democratic classroom practices to make the classroom more of a community for all learners. But governance is only one aspect of what it takes to create a feeling of belonging in a diverse classroom. Many people have experienced a feeling of alienation when they're in the minority. Even when people are granted full rights of citizenship, it doesn't necessarily mean they will experience belonging.

Inclusion, therefore, needs to be a matter of more than placement of students. It ought to mean making a commitment to take whatever steps are necessary to ensure that each and every member of the community feels full membership in the community. There are numerous ways to achieve the goal of inclusion. I have already discussed governance as one strategy. In the next chapter when I discuss usefulness, I will look at how the structuring of interdependence into classroom activities can help enhance students' sense of belonging. But before I close this chapter, here are two additional issues that classroom teachers need to focus on if they are to increase the likelihood of their students feeling full membership in the classroom community:

- Making the classroom friendly to diverse learning styles, and
- Using diversity as an instructional asset.

Using Learning Styles

Research shows that students learn in a variety of ways and come to us with proficiencies and weaknesses in a variety of intelligences (Gardner, 1999; Silver, Strong, & Perini, 2000). Unfortunately, research also shows that many teachers tend to be rigidly consistent in their use of instructional strategies. Too often we teach as though all our students possess the same intelligences and learn the same way we do. For the students who just happen to learn this way and possess strengths that are compatible with our instruction, this is a delightful state of affairs. These students approach class every day feeling that the lesson was designed with them in mind.

But what about a student who is less inclined to enjoy my style of learning or who has to rely on an area of weakness to succeed with the task I've assigned? In my class, that student will likely feel like a fish out of water on a daily basis! I liken this to how I feel when I wear clothes that don't fit. I feel awkward and out of place, and I am consumed by my desire to make a quick exit and change.

When sensitivity to learning styles first surfaced in the early 1980s, many educators thought that the incompatibility of learning style to teaching style would be best remedied by a more skillful placement of students. The rationale was that if students were assigned to a class where the teaching style matched their learning style, they would be comfortable and experience success. On the surface, that strategy appeared to have merit, but closer examination revealed serious flaws. If we teach students only in a single style (one they are comfortable with), we may achieve what appears (on the surface) to be success, but we do so by creating long-term liabilities. If our goal is to empower students for success in adulthood, it is important that they have the capacity to prevail in a wide variety of settings. To serve students well, we must help them develop comfort and skill in a wide range of settings and circumstances. If we attempt to do this without affording the student the occasional pleasant experience that comes from being in his comfort zone, we deny him one essential element of belonging.

Bernice McCarthy (1997) has developed an excellent strategy to address this issue. Her approach involves teachers consciously considering learning style as they prepare units of instruction and then deliberately varying their approach to include each of the most prominent styles. Figure 3.2 illustrates the different types of learning preferences identified by McCarthy.

Figure 3.2
Learning Styles in the McCarthy Model

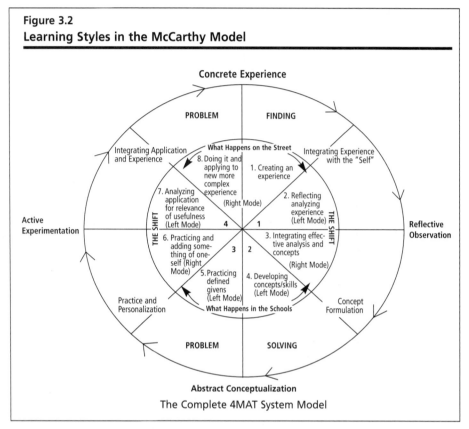

Used by special permission from *The 4MAT system: Teaching and learning with right/left mode techniques* by Bernice McCarthy, EXCEL, Inc., 1987.

Implementation Strategy 3.6 will help you adapt McCarthy's theory to your classroom.

Implementation Strategy 3.6

Making the Classroom Learning-Style Friendly

Either of two approaches ensures that every student regularly experiences lessons that fit just right and also receives opportunities to stretch and develop the skills called for in other types of learning. Choose the approach that best fits your subject or curriculum.

Approach 1

Move around the Learning Style Circle (see Figure 3.2), changing styles on a daily basis. Monday's lesson is designed with the Quadrant 1 learner in mind, Tuesday's will be built upon the style of a Quadrant 2 learner, Wednesday it is time for planning a lesson as though your students were Quadrant 3 learners, and on Thursday the circle is completed with a lesson using the preferences of a Quadrant 4 learner. Following this approach, which is commonly used in secondary schools, ensures that a full week never goes by without all students having a chance to work from their strengths and be within their comfort zone in your class.

Approach 2

Move around the Learning Style Circle on a subject or unit basis. With this approach, frequently used in self-contained classrooms, the teacher designs an entire unit focused on one of the styles. You should be sure that at any given time, instruction in the other subjects emphasizes the other styles. For example: During October, teach science using a Quadrant 1 strategy; for math, use Quadrant 2; in language arts, Quadrant 3; and social studies, Quadrant 4. Following this pattern, you will have enabled every student, every day, to experience instruction that fits while being challenged to work with each of the other styles at least once a day.

Note: It is wise to change styles on a regular basis so students won't begin associating specific learning and teaching styles with particular school subjects.

___

Cultural Diversity and Belonging

Finding their learning styles and intelligences accommodated in class is important to students but is not the only thing that will make them feel at home and comfortable at school. Research in cognitive psychology (Zajonc, 1984; Zajonc & MacIntosh, 1992) and advertising has for years demonstrated that familiarity leads to liking. This phenomenon is true in all aspects of our lives. You've probably noticed that at home you often gravitate toward the couch or a particular chair that you think of as your own. When I return home from a business trip and recognize familiar territory, it triggers an almost euphoric sensation. Students who find their school environment familiar are inclined to find the school an atmosphere they enjoy and in which they feel a sense of belonging. The opposite is also true. If nothing at school looks, smells, or feels familiar, if nothing reminds you of the people and places you most love, and if everything seems foreign to you, it is unlikely that it will be a place where you feel that you belong. More likely it feels like an alien land in which you are but a visitor.

As public schools become more and more diverse, many children feel like aliens in their schools and classrooms. It isn't uncommon for students of color to attend schools where few of the adults look like them or have had any personal experience with their home culture. Many children celebrate holidays and participate in life events at home that personnel at the school may never have even heard about. Therefore, it shouldn't surprise us that, over time, many of these same children come to believe that school has little or nothing to do with them. This belief produces tragic consequences. Researchers (Ogbu, 1991; Gibson & Ogbu, 1991) have documented how many African American boys fear that if they accept the goals of the school, it will mean giving up being black (their culture). That is a choice no young person should ever have to face.

Diversity as an Asset

What can we do about this? To answer that question brings us back to the word *inclusion,* a word discussed throughout this chapter. When we feel included and valued for who we are, we feel that we belong. The key to truly including all students is to bring each student's home culture into the classroom. But this alone is not sufficient to help the minority child feel wanted. It is also important to use strategies that cause all class members to feel that both their learning and their enjoyment are enhanced by the presence of students from different cultures. One such strategy is having students examine academic issues through different cultural lenses. Teachers can help students appreciate diversity by exploring the idea that phenomenon can have different meanings depending on the cultural perspective of the observer. If one of our academic goals is having students become skilled at applying alternative perspectives and alternative problem-solving strategies, we can create opportunities for students from minority cultures to bring something of unique value to their classmates. The very presence of other cultures in the class supplies something worthwhile that would not be there were it not for them.

The benefits of using diversity as an asset serve all students well. Students from the majority culture know they are learning more, and their classes are improved precisely because of the diversity. Inclusion, however, requires more from us than a commitment to celebrate diversity. When schools say they are trying to help students feel at home by celebrating diversity, they are fooling themselves. Simply celebrating diversity says we should be proud of our culture, but it fails to say why. Occasionally, it can even be interpreted as patronizing, implying that differences are quaint, but not significant. However, when we use diversity to broaden and enrich the curriculum, when we use different cultural perspectives in the classrooms to enhance everyone's understanding, then the concrete benefits of diversity and the value of multiculturalism become impossible to miss.

Implementation Strategies 3.7 and 3.8 are approaches that all teachers can use to analyze and adjust their classrooms to be more hospitable to culturally diverse students.

Implementation Strategy 3.7

Conducting a Cultural Audit

A cultural audit will help you determine whether your classroom is a place where students from different cultures are likely to feel a sense of belonging. You can do this four-step activity individually or collectively as a faculty.

Step 1. Record and Collect

On a typical day, tape-record your lessons and collect all the instructional materials you used.

Step 2. Review

Review your lectures, explanations, and discussions and the materials and handouts you used looking for examples or illustrations drawn from nonmajority cultures.

Step 3. Share Your Findings (Optional)

Share the findings with colleagues to see if there is a pattern of multicultural or monocultural perspectives in the school or classroom.

Step 4. Seek Outside Review and Collaboration

If you are not satisfied with the inclusiveness of your instruction and your materials, invite some culturally different parents or school patrons to review your data and to provide suggestions for you on incorporating multiple perspectives into your program.

Implementation Strategy 3.8

Building Diversity into Instruction

Step 1. Review the Goals

List the goals and objectives of the unit you are about to teach or of the course that you are currently teaching.

Step 2. Consider Alternative Perspectives

Ask yourself or inquire of colleagues if the knowledge and skills expected from this unit or class are acquired, understood, or used differently by different cultures or in different parts of the world or, perhaps, even in different parts of our country. If the answer to this question is yes, consider ways that those differences could be used to better help your students understand the concepts or develop the necessary skills.

Step 3. Incorporate Alternative Perspectives

Design your unit plan or course in a way that uses different ways of understanding to produce deeper and broader learning for your students.

The business of school and the job of the knowledge worker is to develop competence. Although having a sense of competence is crucial to motivation, it must be coupled with a sincere sense of belonging. Teachers cannot find fulfillment for an entire career if they are alienated from their peers or from their workplace. Students do not remain engaged or even give themselves the opportunity to develop competence if they come to feel that school is not for them. It is no surprise that when we attend to factors that produce deeper membership at school, we find greater levels of commitment in the work of both teachers and students. Conversely, when we don't, both students and teachers drop out—emotionally, if not physically. Clearly, the price of ignoring the powerful role of belonging is too high a price for society to pay.

Chapter 4

Building Feelings of Usefulness

There is no question that feeling capable (competent) and being comfortable with peers, ourselves, and our communities (belonging) are important. Satisfying those two basic needs, however, isn't enough for people to maintain a passion for their work.

Of all the elements of CBUPO, nothing stimulates motivation as much as the feeling of usefulness. When other people depend on us or when we make noticeable contributions to our community, our self-worth is validated and our self-esteem receives a tremendous boost. The power of usefulness is so great that it even affects our physical well-being.

Power of Usefulness for Teachers

Have you ever wondered why we frequently become ill just in time for vacation? The reason lies in all that is expected of teachers during those hectic weeks before the winter and spring breaks and during the high-pressure closing weeks in June. To meet our responsibilities on those occasions requires our best efforts. Important material must be covered, critical skills need to be acquired, and all the while the clock is running. Add to this scenario the fact that it is highly unlikely that any substitute could effectively work with our students when they are in their hyper prevacation mode. There is no question about it—in the weeks before vacation, classroom teachers are not only needed, but circumstances call for their best performances.

When your work is critical, the body knows it. Your immune system automatically shifts into high gear, and your body becomes nearly impervious to disease. During these stressful periods, you may not be getting the sleep you need, you may not be eating a healthy diet, and you are likely missing the exercise that good health requires. Yet, you remain strong because the situation demands it. Of course, as soon as the crisis abates and the vacation begins, your immune system returns to normal, and you become susceptible to every conceivable opportunistic virus.

Perhaps more than anything else, the power of the innate human need for usefulness explains why dedicated teachers continue to stay with their chosen profession. After all, the compensation is inadequate, if not insulting; the working conditions are frequently far less than satisfactory; society rarely shows teachers the respect they deserve or accords them the status they've earned. Furthermore, most reasonable people question why someone in her right mind would stick with the intellectual and physical demands of teaching.

The power of usefulness is the only plausible explanation for teacher perseverance. Every educator knows that, next to parents, no one has a greater influence on the lives of children and, consequently, the future of our society, than the classroom teacher. Knowing that we are needed (the feeling of usefulness) can make up for a whole lot of negative baggage.

However, the thrust of the standards movement is now placing many teachers at risk of losing their sense of usefulness. In too many places, the implementation of standards-based education has led teachers to feel that they are supposed to leave their creativity at the door. Often they are handed a canned, sometimes even scripted, curriculum. And, in some locales, teachers are given a pacing chart that tells them what to teach and when to teach it. This type of institutional response to standards sends the message that standards-based teaching can be automated to a point that it is teacher-proof.

In these settings, teachers interpret the new job expectation as being "do as you're told." The clear implication is that if you aren't willing to do things the way your supervisor demands or in the manner stipulated by the district, they can find someone else who will. Why should people choose to invest their finite energy into a pursuit that asks them to perform like a robot? Furthermore, when the pay is poor, the working conditions adverse, and respect is absent, is it reasonable to expect someone with other options to stay with it?

Of course, this isn't the only reason policymakers should stop treating teachers like robots or interchangeable parts. Anyone who has worked in a school knows that the search for the teacher-proof curriculum or for an automated program is as futile as it is silly. Teachers will always need to use creativity because human learning is so complex, student diversity is great, and the goal is for all students to succeed. Therefore, our schools must institutionalize regular support opportunities for teachers to feel useful and needed. The best and most appropriate way to accomplish this is to restructure the work of teachers in a manner that encourages them to apply their unique gifts to the complex challenge of universal student success.

Power of Usefulness for Students

Young people need to receive feedback and see concrete evidence of the value of their work as much, if not more, than adults. Happily, some students' need for usefulness is satisfied daily. The spiker on the volleyball team knows that if she isn't there for the big match, her teammates will miss her. The student who has the lead in the spring play knows that if he doesn't show up, the performance will be affected. Likewise, the 3rd grade "student of the week" will tell his parents that it is absolutely crucial that he attend school although he is suffering from a cold. However, not all students have their need for usefulness satisfied at school.

Many years ago, I worked as a teaching assistant for the professor of an introduction to sociology course. I once heard him pose a startling question to a group of freshman students. He asked, "What would be the result if you died tonight?" It was a cold question, but nothing chilled me more than the student responses. Someone suggested that his death would create a vacancy in the dorm. Another said that some professors would experience a reduction in class size. One mentioned that a family, in a faraway part of the state, would deeply mourn the loss of a child. But these students concluded, quite accurately, that "one student more or less" wouldn't make much of a difference.

Reflecting on this event, my comment is "Aside from serving as love objects for their parents and sources of employment for pediatricians and educators, youth serve no real purpose in modern society." Although I can discuss this morbid fact lightheartedly, it is no small problem. Many students drag themselves to school every day, knowing that if they didn't show up, no one would miss them. When people feel that their presence is lacking in value, it is unlikely that they will see a good reason to push themselves to go above and beyond what is expected.

Competition, Cooperation, or Both

In a system based on standards and high-stakes testing, many conclude that it is inevitable that there will be winners and losers. For instance, winning students are promoted, whereas the losers are retained. Schools that score high on the state exam (the winners) receive cash grants and autonomy, whereas the low-scoring schools (the losers) face state takeover. Teachers who are winners receive merit increases, whereas losers face nonrenewal of their contracts. For some fortunate students, specifically those who come to school with the advantages of early success and significant parental support, this type of competitive atmosphere may not be problematic. For a few, it may even be motivational because it is reasonable for those students to conclude, "I can win at this. In the past I've always succeeded, so why shouldn't my streak continue?"

But, what of the student who has struggled or failed and has been relegated to remedial programs? What about the faculty of a school that has historically served an economically disadvantaged community and that, predictably, scores well below the state average? What about the teacher who chooses to work with the most needy children but knows that these are the ones with the greatest likelihood of coming up short? Will a system of winners and losers turn out to be motivational for these people? I suspect not.

Asking professionals to compete with one another in a zero sum game is counterproductive. In the private sector, this truth has been recognized for several years. Many businesses find it more productive to have employees work collaboratively rather than to encourage them to compete against one another. Many teachers find that when they provide cooperative learning opportunities and chances for interdependence in their classrooms, student performance tends to improve. On the surface, it appears cooperation is superior to competition. But this is another area where things may be more complex than they first appear.

Fair Competition

When I taught at the alternative school, it was the height of the Woodstock years. During this time, those drawn to the alternative school movement tended to hold a hostile view of the whole idea of competition. Then, someone came up with the idea of creating a basketball league for the dozen or so alternative schools in the area. The entire alternative school community thought it was a wonderful idea.

We organizers decided that the schools would make each game into a field trip of sorts. The students and teachers from each school would visit each other, tour the facility, and then engage in a good-natured game of basketball. No one suspected that these alienated kids would be motivated with so much competitive zeal.

As it turned out, I was the coach for my school's team. The rude awakening happened at our first event. The players had no interest in a school tour, in sharing milk and cookies with our hosts, or getting to know the teachers. They wanted to play basketball, and they wanted to win! In my entire career, I have never seen a group of kids derive more joy from winning or become more despondent over losing than these alienated alternative school students. After each win, all they wanted to do was practice—after school, in the evenings, even on weekends. After a defeat, I couldn't persuade them to pick up a basketball.

I learned from this experience that competition itself was neither good nor bad. Inherently, it is neither a motivator nor a source of alienation. I started to suspect that there might even be an innate human drive to compete. But the critical issue is that if competition is to be motivational, then the participants must perceive it as fair.

My alternative school students had been in competitive environments before. The mainstream schools they had dropped out of were environments that emphasized competitiveness. Competition was institutionalized through grades, promotion policies, and, informally, through a sharply defined social hierarchy. More important, my alternative school students tended to be the losers in most of these arenas. Consequently, they came to believe that at their previous schools they didn't stand a chance. These experiences led them to make the decision to give up, refuse to compete, and claim that "competition sucks"! However, when these same students experienced what was in their view a level playing field on which they had a reasonable chance to prevail, they lusted for the competition.

Group Versus Individual Competition

Another important element of competition that creates motivation in classrooms is emphasizing team rather than individual, competition. In team sports, such as basketball, it isn't you versus me, it is our team versus your team. This difference is significant because it incorporates the social dimension. Intuitively, being part of a team conveys a sense of belonging and thereby opens opportunities for each member to be useful to a group. The team structure requires that each member play a role in the overall success of the unit. Players know that every member of the team needs me and I need them, if we are to ultimately succeed as a team.

Work in the private sector is generally structured in teams. Employees don't compete against each other. On the contrary, employees work with and help each other solve problems so the work of their team will be good enough to beat the competition. In the corporate sector, this means bettering the competitor in the marketplace.

Using Cooperative Team Learning Structures in the Standards-Based Classroom

In the late 1970s, a group of educators and researchers at Johns Hopkins University developed a series of instructional strategies based on team competition. These classroom strategies were called cooperative team learning (Slavin, 1994).

Slavin and his colleagues at Johns Hopkins helped educators understand the rationale for their model by contrasting the behavior of children in a pickup softball game with the behavior of these same students in class. The social organization of both environments had several similarities. The softball game, like the classroom, contains a truly heterogeneous mix. Some kids have terrific skills, others are just average, and some are rank novices. In the classroom, those same differences can trigger derision or acclaim, but they rarely build solidarity. On the playground, it is just the opposite.

In a pickup game, each team has an equal number of stars, journeymen, and beginners. The success of the team ultimately results from members contributing their best effort. The stars, of course, need to deliver on their strengths. And, if stars can assist the beginners to improve their performance, the entire team benefits. Because of this interdependence, the whole team rejoices as much in the success of its weakest members as it does in the triumph of its stars. Cooperative team learning is a strategy that takes the social structure of the pickup softball game and the fun of participating in fair competition to the academic classroom.

Teams–Games–Tournaments

Teams–Games–Tournaments (TGT) is a structure that is most commonly found in elementary schools. The teacher assigns the students to teams and makes the effort to ensure that each team is as heterogeneous as possible. Let's assume I am doing this for spelling. My first step is to make sure that each team has an equal number of top, middle, and weak spellers. Once students are assigned, they choose a name for their team, perhaps make a team flag, or engage in another activity designed to help provide the group with an identity.

When it is time for spelling, I use the same spelling program, but my students work on their assigned words with their teammates. With this slight shift, spelling time becomes a venue for team practice. On Friday, the day I usually give the weekly spelling quiz, the students enter my room and see it set up for a tournament. I have already placed the tables around the room, and the students are assigned to specific tournament tables. It doesn't take long for the students to see how they were assigned. The top spellers are assigned at tables with other top spellers. The middle achievers have been placed with other middle achievers, and the students who have been struggling with spelling are at tables with other students who have had difficulty with spelling.

At each table, there is a deck of cards with the spelling word on one side and a picture depicting the word on the reverse. Each table also has a pair of dice. Two rolls of the dice determine who goes first. The first player picks up the top card (with the picture up), attempts to spell the word, and then checks the other side to see if the answer is right. If it was correct, the person gets to keep the card. However, if an error is made, the card is returned to the deck. Play continues clockwise around the table until every card is won. Then the students come to my desk to show me how many cards they earned. Each card is worth one point for that competitor's team.

Now, let's stop and consider what it takes for a team to do well. As with softball, the quality of team practice makes a huge difference. If at practice some team members worked in isolation and showed concern only for themselves, then the rest of the team received little or no benefit. However, when the stronger players helped the weaker ones, the likelihood of team success dramatically increased. Even with this incentive to assist team-mates, the stars would be ill advised to simply rest on their lau-rels, since they will be competing against other terrific spellers. With TGT, each team needs each member's best performance for the team to succeed. This inescapable fact gives everyone a chance to feel useful and necessary to team success.

Student Teams Achievement Divisions

The Student Teams Achievement Divisions (STAD) structure is useful at all grade levels. As with Teams–Games–Tournament, the teacher assigns students to heterogeneous teams, based upon the students' past performance, and provides the students an opportunity to develop a team identity. Just as with TGT, the teacher can use whatever program or curriculum had been used in the past. For this example, assume I am a middle school pre-algebra teacher. I begin my unit teaching the material in what-ever manner I deem best. Then, once my students are ready for independent practice, I have them work with their teammates. As was the case with TGT, the purpose of team practice is to prepare for competition. The difference is that with STAD the competition does not take place as a tournament, but as a conventional end-of-unit test.

On test day, my classroom won't look any different from any other class where students are taking an exam. Students will be working individually on their own tests. No talking will be allowed. And, when students complete the test, I collect and score them individually. I record every grade achieved by each student in my grade book, and I use this to determine the course grade. However, before the exam, I compute an average test score based on past exams for each student. This enables me to com-pare each student's end-of-the-unit test score to the previous average achieved by the same student. I then record any points above the students' previous averages as points for their team.

Let's now look at how and why this structure works. The stu-dents who in the past had been the weaker students—perhaps with mere 60 percent averages—have the potential to become their team's most valuable player. After all, a perfect score will be worth a whopping 40 points. Conversely, the top students on the team—with, say, impressive 92 percent averages—won't be scoring many points unless they turn in truly outstanding performances. To make things both fair and motivational for top achievers, many teachers award a substantial bonus for a perfect score.

Jigsaw II

In this cooperative team learning structure, the content to be studied is divided into pieces. As with all cooperative learning structures, Jigsaw II students are assigned to heterogeneous teams. For this example, assume that I teach high school geography and the class is studying Brazil. I first look over my unit, reflect on the content I believe should be covered, and review the available materials. After this review, I determine that I can evenly divide this unit into history, government, culture, and ecology; then I prepare a comprehensive study guide. The guide directs the learner to the appropriate material and outlines the activities necessary for learning the material and developing mastery of the key concepts. I divide the study guide into four parts, one for each of the four unit components. Within their teams, each student draws a card listing one of the unit components and is responsible for teaching that material to the other team members.

At this point, I provide students with substantial time, perhaps a week or more, to independently acquire the skills and gain the knowledge indicated on their portion of the study guide. At the end of the allotted period, I assign each student to an expert group (one expert group per study guide topic). Typically, an expert group has at least one member from each team. These expert groups gather to help each other as they prepare for the responsibility of teaching their portion of the Brazil unit to the rest of their team. To effectively fulfill this responsibility, the time they spend in the expert group can be of great importance, as this is their best opportunity to be sure they have sufficient mastery of the material.

After I have given ample time for the work of the expert groups, it is time for team learning. Team learning generally takes several days, as each student expert teaches the other team members his portion of the unit. After team study time, each student individually completes a test or project on Brazil. Just as I did with STAD, I post and record all student points in my grade book. And again, as with STAD, teams earn points based upon the degree of improvement made by each group member.

The Common Threads

Each of these three learning structures has the following characteristics in common:

- Each team member influences team performance through individual efforts.

- The team competes as a unit. Success is applauded based on the result of group work, not on one student winning over another.

- Contributions from individual team members make for group success; however, students are individually accountable for their own performance.

There is much to commend the three cooperative team learning structures (TGT, STAD, and Jigsaw II), which were developed at Johns Hopkins University. However, those structures are not the only way to incorporate the characteristics of the cooperative classroom. Implementation Strategy 4.1 takes you through the steps for developing an accountable cooperative learning unit.

Implementation Strategy 4.1

Developing an Accountable Cooperative Learning Unit

Step 1.

Choose a unit of study that links to the standards you expect to teach.

Step 2.

Determine what specific skills and knowledge your students must acquire.

Step 3.

Decide how to structure the learning of this material so that every student can make a contribution to the success of other students in the class.

Step 4.

Consider how you can structure the learning to enable each student to see and appreciate the contribution she is making to the success of others.

Step 5.

Decide how you can assess the performance of each student in relation to the goals and objectives of the unit.

Step 6.

Consider how you can ensure that individual students are held accountable for personal success and contributions to the learning of other class members.

Useful Work

The usefulness of the work one does has a great influence on its motivational value. But, what makes work useful? There are two aspects of useful work. The first pertains to the value of the work in the marketplace. In modern society, people pay for work they value. Consequently, the value of the goods and services a person produces isn't based upon an arbitrary supervisor's assessment, but upon the value placed on the product by an independent consumer.

The second type of usefulness pertains to the social value of the work. Some products and services make the world, the community, and life itself better for others. The value of this work lies in the knowledge that had this work not been done, real human needs would not have been met or not met as well. Charitable work fits this definition. When people are in possession of evidence that their work is valued, it inevitably confirms that they have made a difference.

The two types of value that are found in useful work stand in sharp contrast to what students call schoolwork. Most students see a dichotomy: real-world work and schoolwork. The primary difference is that they produce schoolwork for an audience of one (the teacher) and its purpose is getting credit or a grade. Furthermore, once the teacher awards the grade, the work no longer has any real value. This dichotomy is reinforced by the fact that the tasks that constitute schoolwork are rarely seen outside the school setting. Other than when taking the written portion of the driving test, most adults never confront multiple-choice questions or any other sort of timed exam after graduating. Is it any wonder, then, that when we teachers assign schoolwork, we often hear our students asking these questions:

- "How much do you want?"
- "What do I have to do to get an *A*?"
- "Is this required?"
- "Why do we have to do this?"
- "How long should it be?"

These questions wouldn't make much sense if the student was developing a product for sale in the marketplace. In those circumstances, the answer would be clear: "The work has to be good enough to satisfy the consumer's desires." In the case of service work, the answer would be, "It needs to be good enough to meet the client's need." This difference in assessment criteria explains why many teachers find getting good work from students a bit like coaxing cooperation from a mule.

Authentic Learning and Assessment

Increasingly teachers are seeing the benefits of narrowing or eliminating the distinction between real-world work and schoolwork. This can be accomplished through the use of authentic learning and authentic assessment.

The term *authentic* is well chosen because what is authentic is real. Authentic work is work that results in a product. An authentic product is something that

- stands by itself, apart from its creator, and
- can be appreciated for its own innate worth.

Authentic work has always been produced in schools, but not in all of the disciplines. A painting done by an art student is a piece of authentic work. So is the play put on by the drama class, the canned food drive organized by the leadership class, and the auto-body work done by the shop class. What each of these examples has in common is that

- The end product approximates items that are valued and paid for in the real world, and

- The essential quality of the work can be assessed by anyone willing to examine it.

When you witness the pride exhibited by the student performing a solo at the choir concert, you can readily see the intrinsic benefit of success with authentic work. Two current trends in education lend themselves well to our efforts to make academic work more authentic: (1) problem-based learning (Delisle, 1997; Torp & Sage, 2002), and (2) service learning (Kinsley & McPherson, 1995).

Problem-Based Learning

Beyond the fact that schoolwork often involves tasks that are absent from real-world work, it is often built upon an unnatural separation of the disciplines. For example, we often ask students to learn language arts independent of social studies and science, and math is rarely taught in conjunction with health. Problem-based learning (PBL) is a strategy with significant potential to overcome both of these inherent problems with single-discipline schoolwork. For many years, beginning with colleges of medicine, PBL has been a popular instructional strategy in undergraduate and graduate-level education.

The essence of PBL is presenting to students a real problem that people or communities are grappling with and asking the students to craft a thoughtful solution to the problem. Obviously, there is never a shortage of problems that could be posed to our students:

- A recovery plan for an endangered species,
- The creation of safer playground equipment,

- Developing a successful antismoking campaign, or

- Reducing domestic dependence on foreign oil.

Once students choose a problem, with some gentle guidance from the teacher, they can begin conducting the necessary research to develop a deep understanding of the related issues. This background is critical if they are to succeed in designing a solution worthy of community or professional consideration. Often the last step in the PBL process is having the student present a solution or proposal to the people with decision-making authority.

As a teacher, you'll ask where can I find the time to engage students in these types of projects when I still have to prepare them for the state test and help them gain proficiency on the mandated standards? The answer? Regardless of how good or motivating an instructional program might be, if implementing it produces negative consequences for the students, it is wrong to do so. If we are to hold students accountable on high-stakes tests, then preparing them for those tests must be our top priority. The only responsible way to do both is to find a way to embed the mandated standards into the student's PBL work. Academic coaches can use the following approach at any grade level, although a greater amount of teacher guidance will be needed when using it with younger students.

Embedding Mandated Standards in Problem-Based Learning

While preparing students for assessment on mandated standards, I try to harness the motivational value of problem-based learning by emphasizing these four steps:

1. Inform the students of the standards or competencies that they are expected or required to master by the end of the school year (course).

2. Point out that there are many ways to acquire those skills—some clearly more fun than others.

3. Tell them that I know they enjoy authentic learning, and I will make every effort to effectively teach and have them acquire the required standards while they are working with real-world issues.

4. Caution them that any skills not developed to high levels of proficiency will be, by necessity, the focus of intense drill and practice two months before the exam.

If you decide to use this strategy for embedding standards into authentic learning, then I suggest that you post the applicable standards throughout the classroom. Prominently posting standards is important for two reasons: First, it ensures that all students can see the targets that they will be accountable for reaching. Second, it reminds the students of the incentive for incorporating the required standards into their PBL projects.

After orienting the students to the connections between PBL and the acquisition of standards (by completing the four steps), it is time to get started. Early in the PBL process it is wise to have students develop a detailed work plan. During the preparation of the work plan, ask your students to carefully review the standards for which they are accountable and to structure the acquisition and demonstration of those skills into their work plans. Remind them that they have two good reasons to take the embedding process seriously. First, they will have to master the standards; second, they can either do it in the context of work they find meaningful or as mundane preparation for the exam.

Implementation Strategy 4.2 lays out the sequence for implementing problem-based learning in a standards-based classroom.

Implementation Strategy 4.2

Implementing Problem-Based Learning

Step 1. Establish the Focus

Determine the overriding focus for the project (the general thrust of the work). For example, depending on the curriculum, it could be an area such as ecology, health, or government.

Step 2. Establish Parameters

Decide if you want all students to work on the same specific problem (e.g., a recovery plan for the spotted owl) or choose from a larger set of problems (e.g., animal recovery, sustainable forests, recycling).

Step 3. Review the Appropriate Standards

Review the standards assigned to your grade level to determine which ones can most effectively be embedded in the search for solutions and the development of proposals to solve this PBL problem.

Step 4. Establish Expectations

Decide on the attributes of the expected finished product (a written proposal, a PowerPoint presentation, an oral presentation) and who will be the audience and assessor of the final product (e.g., the teacher, the city council, the state ecology department, a professor at the state university).

Step 5. Introduce the Problem

Introduce the problem to the students in a way that helps them see the rich complexity of the issue. Also convey that you have confidence that they can craft a successful solution, given their creativity and hard work.

Step 6. Conduct Research

With your guidance, have the students do some background investigation into the issues surrounding their problem.

Step 7. Develop Work Plans

Have your students develop work plans. Depending on their experience with developing work plans, you might want to provide less-experienced students with a detailed format for the plan while giving more experienced students an open-ended opportunity to construct their own.

Step 8. Invite Students to Embed the Standards

Once the students develop their work plan, engage them in a discussion on which standards could be covered in the course of their work. If the students don't mention items on your list (Step 3), this is the appropriate time for you to bring them up.

Step 9. Provide a Timeline

Inform the students of a timeline for completion of the project, the format you expect the final product to be in, and the audience for their presentation.

Step 10. Provide Guidance

Be there as a guide as they pursue their work.

Step 11. Assess the Students

Following the completion of the PBL project, assess the students on the grade-level standards and skills that were embedded in their work plan.

Step 12. Report Results of the Assessment

If student performance on the embedded standards demonstrates proficiency, then you just need to congratulate the students, cross the standard off the lists posted in the classroom, and remind them that they have one less thing to work on as part of that dreary drill and kill test preparation.

Service Learning

To stimulate student feelings of usefulness, it is hard to imagine anything better than service learning. The notion of connecting community service to school expectations got a boost when Ernest Boyer (1983) in his landmark book, *High School,* argued that community service ought to become a new Carnegie unit required for high school graduation.

The rationale we hear most frequently for requiring community service is a moral one, which is justified as well as logical. After all, who would question the inherent good of giving back to your community? It has also been argued quite eloquently that the act of helping others builds character. Today, parents and the larger community are asking schools to play a more prominent role in character development. As meritorious as all this appears, basing an argument for mandatory service learning solely on moral and ethical grounds provides educators with a tough choice. Should we siphon finite time that is already in short supply and that is vitally needed for academic preparation and spend it on a worthwhile, yet nonacademic, endeavor? Fortunately, this may be one of those instances where we can have our cake and eat it, too.

As with problem-based learning, bringing the community and the real world into the classroom doesn't necessarily have to mean reducing our academic focus. With deliberate and creative planning, community service can simultaneously serve academic, ethical, and motivational purposes.

To get the most out of a service-learning experience, follow these three guidelines:

1. The work should be ongoing,

2. The work needs to draw upon the student's preexisting talents and skills, and

3. The work must engage the student in the development of valuable new skills, insights, or knowledge.

Let's now consider the rationale for each of these guidelines.

1. The work needs to be ongoing. Many teachers have had their students engage in charitable work. I applaud this effort. Canned food drives have fed many hungry people, and contributions to UNICEF have helped thousands, if not millions, of children in poverty. Although something good and essential is accomplished for the recipients of these charitable efforts, students learn little. The students who won the pizza party for bringing in the most food only remember how hard they found it to remind classmates to bug their parents for contributions. I don't wish to disparage the result of these programs, but it is unlikely that through this type of charitable work the students developed a deep understanding of how and why their work made a difference in the lives of real people. The work is largely episodic and the recipients far away. Feelings of usefulness are most powerfully built when you see evidence of the influence that your efforts are having on others. Ongoing work affords students a chance to observe the specific changes that occurred as a direct result of their effort.

Service opportunities that students can be engaged in on an ongoing basis are unlimited. Examples range from students tutoring other students, adopting the residents at a local retirement home, to taking on the responsibility for the development and maintenance of a neighborhood park.

What each of these opportunities has in common is that they enable the service providers (the students) to observe the effects of their contribution over time.

Studies (Gaustad, 1993) on cross-age tutoring have shown that tutors tend to gain at least as much academically as their tutees. As all teachers know, the best way to learn something is to teach it. But it is likely more than that. These gains are also the result of the boost in self-esteem that occurs when older students see the gains they helped the younger students achieve. It is one thing to go out and sing for the residents at a nursing home, but quite another to establish a relationship with a resident who looks forward to the visits, hangs student artwork in her room, and talks to others about her young friend. Similarly, policing the grounds of a park is one thing, but showing off the plantings, the flowerbeds, and the playground equipment that you personally raised funds for, designed, and still maintain conveys a different message. That message is, "Without me this would or could not have occurred."

2. The work needs to draw on the student's preexisting talents and skills. True service provides someone, or some community, with something they couldn't have had or done as efficiently for themselves. If we ask our students to do something for which they lack the skills or know-how, then the effort that we need to expend supervising them as they do their work can exceed the benefits provided. Furthermore, if one of our main goals is reinforcing feelings of usefulness, consider that what makes the students useful is the fact that they possess the skills and knowledge to accomplish the work.

3. The work must engage the student in the development of valuable skills, insights, or knowledge. Although there is much to be said for doing mundane and menial work for the benefit of others, the school day is not the time nor is school the place for those efforts. And, while it is certainly humbling to do servile work for those in need, taking away from a student's finite learning time without gaining a return in academic proficiency is too high a price to pay. So how can we structure valuable academic learning into a service learning expectation?

One excellent approach is to embed academic learning into service learning as with PBL activities (see Implementation

Strategy 4.2, p. 96). Implementation Strategy 4.3 provides a set of guidelines for the use of service learning in a standards-based setting.

Implementation Strategy 4.3

Designing a Service Learning Program

Step 1. Select a Project

Brainstorm potential ongoing projects that would make a real difference in the lives of people in your community. Decide if you want all students to participate in the same service project. Although there is benefit in providing a degree of choice, there is also merit in having one big project that the classroom (as a community) takes on as a group.

Step 2. Review the Appropriate Standards or Expected Products

Review the standards assigned to your grade level. Decide which ones you can embed into this service work. Decide what products are to be produced or the results that are likely to be obtained from engagement with this work (e.g., a work of art, the development of listening skills, knowledge about careers).

Step 3. Introduce the Project

Introduce the project to your students. Help them see the critical needs that they will meet, paying particular attention to what would likely happen if someone did not provide this service.

Step 4. Develop Work Plans and Embed Standards

Have the students develop work plans. You probably want to provide a format or worksheet as a guide to building a work plan. Once you and the students have developed the work plan, engage students in a discussion about which (grade-level) standards will come into play in the course of providing this service. Should there be some items on your list (Step 2) that didn't appear on theirs, this is the appropriate time for you to discuss them.

Step 5. Review Benefits and Possible Outcomes

Ask the students to describe any additional benefits they believe the recipients of the service or they themselves will obtain from this work. Discuss with students how to collect data (evidence) to document those benefits.

Step 6. Monitor and Support

Be a guide to students as they perform their service. Be sure that the students collect data and artifacts on the results of the work. Have students produce a final written, oral, or visual project that details their experience and the results of their service work.

It is amazing the number of academic skills that we can embed into real-world work. For example, a public alternative middle school in Clearwater, Florida, delivers an entire comprehensive middle school curriculum by having the students maintain and run a nine-hole public golf course. Apparently, the only thing that limits a combination of academic and authentic service learning is a lack of creativity.

Reinforcing the Teacher's Sense of Usefulness

The development of the feelings of competence, belonging, usefulness, and potency is not separate and discrete. The activities introduced in chapters 2 and 3 directly affect a teacher's sense of usefulness.

Looking at the value your teaching has added to student learning (Implementation Strategy 2.1, p. 26) reveals a great deal about the value of your work and the usefulness of your efforts. Likewise, participating in an internal consultancy program (Implementation Strategy 3.5, p. 71) and seeing your colleagues adopt and adapt specific innovative instructional processes that you developed cannot help but enhance your feelings of usefulness.

As a teacher, however, you deserve evidence of the difference you make in student lives. A few other mechanisms can assist you in seeing the incredible influence you have on students' lives.

Glatthorn's Model of Curriculum

Allan Glatthorn (1987) created a most helpful way to look at curriculum. His view of school curricula is illustrated in Figure 4.1.

Glatthorn asks us to think of the curriculum as having three parts. The first part, the mastery curriculum, corresponds to the state and district standards. Teachers expect students to possess these skills and attributes by the end of the grade or instructional period. But, as all teachers, students, parents, and community members know, the sum of the mastery curriculum is not all that we want children to take from their schooling.

The second part, the organic curriculum, contains those skills and attributes that teachers want all students to develop but that can't be taught or assigned to a particular class or grade level. Attributes such as a love of reading, an appreciation of art, perseverance, respect for others, and the ability to access information are examples of elements that make up the organic curriculum.

If you try to assign an organic curriculum objective to a particular grade level, you will see how much this differs from the mastery curriculum. For example, what if we assigned love of reading to the 3rd grade? In fact, suppose we said it was to be covered during the first six weeks of school. Would anyone think

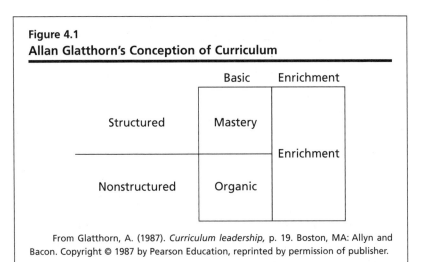

Figure 4.1
Allan Glatthorn's Conception of Curriculum

	Basic	Enrichment
Structured	Mastery	Enrichment
Nonstructured	Organic	

From Glatthorn, A. (1987). *Curriculum leadership,* p. 19. Boston, MA: Allyn and Bacon. Copyright © 1987 by Pearson Education, reprinted by permission of publisher.

that by Thanksgiving break the students would have developed a lifelong love of reading? Of course not. Although the objectives of the organic curriculum are every bit as important as those found in the mastery curriculum, they are developed over the student's entire school career. Unfortunately, it is rare that anyone assesses student growth and development with the organic curriculum. Consequently, the acts of teaching that may inspire significant growth in these areas often aren't recognized. Worse yet, the teachers who are expending the effort to achieve these successes are denied an opportunity to see the effect they are having on student development.

Implementation Strategy 4.4 is an approach that is helpful in capturing a greater range of the development you are actually producing with your students.

Implementation Strategy 4.4

Documenting Success with the Organic Curriculum

Step 1. Review the Mastery Curriculum

Look at the list of standards and objectives assigned to your class or grade level by the state, district, and school (the mastery curriculum).

Step 2. Identify the Organic Curriculum

In addition to the mastery curriculum, what else would you want students to develop as a consequence of their experience in this class and school, or as a consequence of their immersion in this mastery curriculum?

Step 3. Decide on the Assessment Process

For each item on your list (the elements of the organic curriculum), ask yourself: "How might I document the growth that is occurring?" For example, if I want to see an increase in my student's recreational reading, a log of their reading of nonassigned material would be a source of data. If I want to see the degree to which my students are developing perseverance, my observations of their behavior when working with complex multistep problems and data obtained from interviews with parents might provide insights into the changes that are occurring.

Step 4. Collect and Analyze the Data

Collect the data you identified in Step 3 in a systematic and regular way. At the end of the year, make a list of your students and note the growth that each one has demonstrated (on the organic objectives) as a consequence of their experience in your class.

Step 5. Take Stock

Over the years, keep a running total of the lives that your work has forever altered.

Let's return to Glatthorn's conception of curriculum (Figure 4.1, p. 103). In addition to the mastery and organic curricula, there is another curriculum—the enrichment curriculum. This curriculum refers to learning that teachers value enough to teach (offer), but it is learning that we neither require nor expect every student to accomplish. In secondary schools, these courses are labeled *electives*. Electives are valuable academic experiences that are worthy of credit, but students only experience them as a result of individual interest or need. It is important to note that electives are not the only, nor should they be the primary, place where students encounter the enrichment curriculum. Students experience the enrichment curriculum even when they do not select classes.

I have yet to meet the teacher who teaches only what is in the book or contained in the curriculum manual. Teachers bring their interests, passions, experiences, and perspectives into their classroom. Furthermore, these intangibles are frequently what students remember most about the time they spend in our classrooms. Modeling is a teacher's most powerful teaching tool. Students remember and learn from our unique personalities and interests every bit as much as they learn from the materials we use. If we constructed a Venn diagram showing the content taught by two teachers who were both rigorously and successfully teaching to the state standards, it would look like Figure 4.2.

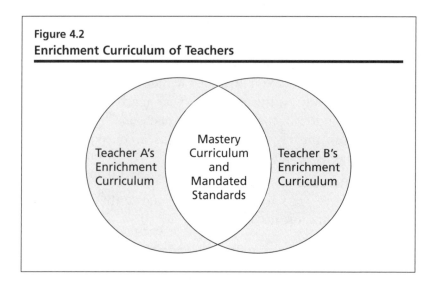

Figure 4.2
Enrichment Curriculum of Teachers

The white area corresponds to the mastery or state curriculum. The students in both classes receive a comparable focus on these. The shaded areas represent the enrichment curriculum. This is the material, the insights, the knowledge, and the skills that students experience only because they had Teacher A or Teacher B. Although this material isn't required, it certainly enriches the students' lives. Implementation Strategy 4.5 helps you to acknowledge and trace the effects that your enrichment curriculum has had on your students.

Implementation Strategy 4.5

Taking Stock of the Enrichment Curriculum

Step 1. Review What You've Taught

Review the lesson plans for a course or unit you recently completed. Identify the key learning experiences provided for students and what you hoped they would gain from each of those experiences.

Step 2. Categorize the Content

Next to each item indicate with the letter M if it was part of the required mastery curriculum or with an E if it was part of the enrichment curriculum (something you elected to include).

Don't be concerned that often objectives of the organic curriculum also show up as enrichment. Frequently, the best way to teach the habits and perspectives of the organic curriculum is through our unique enrichment activities.

Step 3. Review the Evidence

Ask yourself: "What evidence did I collect on my students' learning of those objectives marked with an *E*?" Summarize this evidence. This measures the things that your students gained that they would not have gained were it not for you!

Step 4. Make a Commitment

If you didn't gather the evidence needed to answer the question (Step 3), ask yourself: "What data might I collect next year to demonstrate the effect my teaching of the enrichment curriculum had on my students?" Make a commitment to collect that data.

Implementation Strategy 4.5 could also be used, in a modified format, by an entire school faculty. Just as no two teachers cover the identical content, the student experience is qualitatively different in every school in a district. Taking a good look at what students experience only through their good fortune of attending your school should prove to be a powerful source of collective satisfaction for the entire faculty.

The Intersection of Motivational Needs

In Chapter 2, I discussed using assessment data as a method for taking stock of the effects our teaching has on our students (Implementation Strategy 2.1, p. 26). Likewise, Implementation Strategies 4.4 and 4.5 (p. 104 and p. 106) provide additional validation of our teaching competence. By engaging in a helping occupation, teachers are afforded a chance for a wonderful double-dip in motivation. When we are good at our work, it means we are successfully helping others.

Before addressing potency, it is worth another look at ways we can make useful contributions to the professional work of our colleagues. Figure 4.3 contains a partial list of programs, committees, and structures that have been used in many schools, are facilitated by teachers, and have resulted in improved teaching and learning, as well as enhancing job satisfaction.

When we consider what it takes to reinforce a teacher's sense of usefulness, it is important to consider the distinction between a professional organization and a simple workplace. In a simple workplace, all that is expected of the workers, both personally and by their supervisors, is that they do the job. If they do well with their assignment, they can rightfully feel useful. After all, they did their part.

But, in a professional organization, your sense of pride and satisfaction comes from the finished product (i.e., the

---

Figure 4.3
Building-Based Teacher Support Programs

Multidisciplinary Team handles special needs referrals and consultation with teachers

Shared Governance Committee makes certain that decision-making processes are working effectively

Technology Cadre is the conduit for information, support, and training on instructional uses of technology

Curriculum Coordinating Council takes responsibility to ensure effective articulation is occurring

Assessment and Testing Committee works to provide or facilitate the development of assessments that are tied to the curriculum

Peer Coaching Program pairs of teachers observe and confer with one another in an effort to enhance instruction skills

Teacher Assistance Program provides confidential, nonjudgmental support to teachers on any issue that is impairing their ability to be successful and satisfied with work

New Teacher Induction Program focuses on helping teachers new to the building or new to the profession get off to a smooth start

Professional Development Committee provides or arranges to have professional development activities for faculty that are responsive to faculty needs

Social Committee focuses on maintaining a positive interpersonal climate

Scheduling Task Force works with administration on construction of the master schedule

Guidance Committee assists the guidance staff in providing supportive academic services

well-educated student), not just from doing your part. Anyone who has done good work in a low-performing school knows how frustrating it can feel. You start to feel like the little boy who tries to repair the dike by placing his finger in a hole. Rather than building CBUPOs, even when people do great work in dysfunctional professional organizations, they feel frustrated. For that reason, it is worth taking the time to look over the list of programs and services in Figure 4.3 and ask if these services are being effectively provided to the teaching staff at your school, either by faculty members or others. If the answer is yes, then you are likely working in a functional professional organization.

If the answer is no, it may be a good time to take decisive action. Certainly, no busy teacher looks for additional work. The old adage "If it ain't broke, don't fix it" also applies to the work of teachers. But, if a service or a program will truly help teachers in your school to be more effective and to experience greater job satisfaction, and it isn't available, something needs to happen. If professionals can provide these types of services for each other (i.e., professional development, collaborative planning, or developing interventions for challenged students), it can be satisfying to play a part in providing those services for your colleagues. Yes, it may mean extra work, but this type of work enhances your feelings of competence, belonging, and usefulness. Furthermore, this type of work may also give a tremendous boost to your feelings of potency.

"A life spent helping others is a life well spent" is a particularly apt adage for teachers. We are fortunate to have been called to a profession where our every action provides a benefit for students, society, and our collective futures. Never forget that your life is being well spent.

Chapter 5

Producing Feelings of Potency

E very element of competence, belonging, usefulness, potency, and optimism influences motivation, but nothing is more critical than the feeling of personal and collective potency.

Early Learning and Potency

Fortunately, some children experience success in their first days at school. My two daughters had a wonderful preschool experience. Donna Hargraeves, their teacher at the local Parish Montessori School, structured success into each child's experience. She gently guided them to activities for which they were developmentally ready, and they enthusiastically worked at tasks until they reached mastery. She filled each school day with opportunities for them to do things that they were unable to do the day before. My visits to the classroom were opportunities for my girls to strut with pride. They would take me from station to station, showing off what they now could do.

My children were blessed with other marvelous teachers who, rather than simply telling them that they were good or smart, provided a classroom structure where the students experienced concrete success with tasks and skills that they perceived as challenging. Consequently, my high school daughter and her 6th grade sister don't shy away from challenges; rather, they seek them out. They view difficult work as providing an opportunity for them to experience that wonderful feeling of competence. But imagine for a moment if the opposite had been true. What if Ellisa and Emma had repeatedly experienced failure at school? What if each task and challenge presented to them was simply another opportunity to fail and further doubt their abilities as students? How would we expect them to approach challenging and demanding work? Would we expect enthusiasm, anticipation, and perseverance? I think not.

We need to understand that the student who appears to avoid every challenge, puts forth minimal effort, and readily gives up may not be a reluctant learner or an obstinate kid. It is more likely that this student has made a logical and rational calculation. The student has internalized the truth that the greatest predictor of the future is the past. If, in the past, effort has repeatedly produced failure, why should the student now expect anything different?

The Teacher's Need for Potency

If the satisfaction of this most basic need—experiencing personal potency—is denied to a classroom teacher, the results can be devastating. I firmly believe that the feeling of impotence, increasingly internalized by many teachers, results in a sense of defeatism on the part of many faculties and is the greatest single problem facing education today.

Consider that teachers entered the profession believing that they could and would be helping students develop academic skills and gain knowledge that would later empower them as adults. We believed we could succeed in developing traits of character to help our students grow into good citizens. Why else would any of us have entered such a demanding profession, where compensation, appreciation, and status are so low? Now, think of how often we hear colleagues make these comments:

- "Let's be realistic. There is only so much we can expect of these kids."

- "Given the homes these students come from, they will never meet these high standards."

- "Without more administrative support, this is the best we can do."

These statements are expressions of impotence and a lack of efficacy. Feelings of impotence arise from what psychologists refer to as an external locus of control. Experience has taught these teachers that student success is outside their control; they perceive other factors—factors they cannot influence—as playing a much more significant role in the success of their students. What a sad state this impotency creates. Certainly, it is sad for the children, whose teachers begin the school year having already given up or having lowered their expectations. But it is also tragic for the teachers themselves. Just a few years ago, they joined the ranks of a profession with high hopes, only to have them dashed and replaced by an overpowering feeling of hopelessness.

Certainly, issues such as poverty, the absence of early learning experiences, living in dysfunctional families, and a lack of parental support are formidable obstacles. Certainly, they conspire to make the work of the teacher far more difficult than any of us would like. But, once we begin to believe that they preordain the outcome for our students, we have relegated ourselves to the role of mere babysitters.

In facing the critical problem of feelings of impotence, we teachers need not despair. Students who lack self-confidence and teachers who think the battle is lost before they begin can have those perspectives turned around.

Connecting Behavior to Results

Often students fail to see the connection between their actions and the consequences of those actions. When it comes to behavior, they seem to have no sense of cause and effect. If we want students to take pride in their success, they first need to see that success or failure is not the result of luck but is the consequence of the choices they make.

The inability of some students to see the connection between behavior and results was driven home to me during my first job as a school administrator. I was a high school vice principal with primary responsibility for handling discipline. Furthermore, I worked in a severely disadvantaged community where, unfortunately, the students had few successful adult role models.

When a teacher sent students to my office, I generally followed a ritual. I asked the students to write their understanding of what happened to cause their removal from class. This activity kept the students productively occupied for the remainder of the period, and provided me with information that could be used later in the day when I talked with the teacher. Soon I noted an interesting pattern. What the students perceived as the cause of the difficulty often bore little resemblance to the perception of the teachers or even the actual behavior that had precipitated their office referral.

For example, when a student shouted a disrespectful epithet at the teacher and was consequently removed from class, the student might write,

> The teacher hates me. She is always looking for a reason to come down on me. All I did was ask John what page we were on, and she got all over my case. That's why I got mad. She's the one who caused the problem in the first place!

What I began to realize was that many students had a problem seeing the connection between their behavior and the consequences of that behavior. These students were inclined to think that the way to get rich was by winning the lottery; the way to do well in school was to be born smart; and the trick to becoming a good athlete was having innate talent. These students failed to see that hard work and perseverance far better predict future financial success than picking winning lottery numbers. If they didn't recognize that results are the consequences of their actions, they certainly didn't realize that successful students were actually the beneficiaries of their hard and focused work, which included doing their homework and asking for help when needed. These students were honestly unaware that world-class athletes spend hours at practice, in the weight room, and following the advice of their coaches.

Given the view that the things that happen to us are out of our control and the belief that the difficulties that arise are the fault of other people or the consequence of bad luck, the students' perspectives weren't illogical. In my role as vice principal, my job was to help students learn from their mistakes and make better behavior choices in the future. I soon realized that I had to find a way to break through the belief that they were merely innocent bystanders as external events swirled around and conspired against them.

Behavior Recognition

I used a strategy that I call behavior recognition. In the case of the disrespectful student, it was clear to me and to the teacher that it was the student's decision to shout the epithet that created the problem. The student, however, honestly didn't recognize the relationship between his act and the outcome. I used the strategy of having the student tell me, in sequence, every single event that had transpired. While the student talked, I wrote on my office whiteboard precisely what the student said. In this case, my notes might have read something like this:

1. She told us we were supposed to be working quietly on our own work.

2. She told us which page each group should be working on.

3. I knew which group I was in, but didn't hear the page our problems were on.

4. So, I asked John what page we were supposed to be working on.

5. She got mad and glared at me.

6. She came over to my desk and said she was tired of having to remind me to follow the rules.

7. I said, "I was just trying to do the work."

8. She said, "It would help if you paid attention when I gave the instructions."

9. I got mad because she is always yelling at me.
10. Then I told her to . . .

Then, I ask the student to go through each one of the steps and to tell me what specific thing resulted in an office referral. The student read the list and realized that none of the things that occurred in steps 1–9 would cause the teacher to send him out of the room. He wasn't removed for being mad at the teacher or because the teacher was mad at him, or even for asking John for help. With my guidance, the student ultimately recognized on his own that it was his choice to shout the expletive that caused him to be kicked out.

At that time, I ask, "What could you have done at that point (following Step 8) that might have kept you from being sent to the office and facing this suspension?" Occasionally requiring some prodding, the student would cite several alternatives:

- "I could have just sat there and done nothing the whole period."

- "I could have asked her to let me go see my counselor and complained to the counselor."

- "I could have just sat there getting madder and madder."

At this stage, I didn't concern myself with how productive any of these alternative behaviors were. That was not my primary goal. What mattered most to me was for the student to see who had the control over the ultimate outcome.

Tightening the Feedback Loop

The behavior recognition strategy is also helpful when teachers observe a pattern of substandard performance on long-term academic projects. Everyone remembers those first days of kindergarten and 1st grade. Each day ended with carrying home a completed piece of work with a star from the teacher. In the evening each student could say to parents, "This is what I did today. See, I did a good job!"

As students move up the grades, the feedback loop, that is, the time between doing the work and receiving an assessment, steadily increases. Two weeks might be spent studying material before taking the unit test. A teacher may assign a research paper three weeks before it is due. As teachers, many of us have had students who fell off the track almost as soon as we made the assignment. Perhaps they became confused, yet didn't ask for help, or they didn't make good use of class or library time. Yet, when they received the unacceptable grade on their test or project, they would claim we gave them a bad grade. It was the teacher who *gave* the grade, not their work, or the lack thereof, that was responsible. These students, the ones who haven't yet begun to see the connection between behavior and results, may actually believe their assertions. After all, they did stay up late the night before working hard to pull together the best project they could at the last minute.

Teachers can do two things to help students who have an external locus of control to understand how their choices ultimately contribute to success or lead to failure. The first is to follow the same steps I used with the misbehaving student: Have the student retrace all the events that led up to the ultimate outcome. A second and often more productive approach is to shorten the feedback loops for these students. This does not mean avoiding long-term projects and extended units. Rather it means building numerous, perhaps even daily, benchmarks or mileposts that the teacher and student can monitor. The use of Implementation Strategy 5.1 can help your students learn to recognize the connection between behavior and results.

Implementation Strategy 5.1

Tightening the Feedback Loop

Think of the next long-term (1–3 week) project you will have your students complete. Use this project to help your low-efficacy students learn to connect behavior to results.

Step 1. Conduct a Task Analysis

Break down the project into a sequential list of tasks. The list should include everything the students must learn, do, or accomplish in order to produce a high-quality finished product.

Step 2. Monitor the Work

Ask yourself, "What evidence would clearly demonstrate to me and to the student that they had accomplished each one of the tasks detailed above?" Then ask yourself, "How can this evidence be timely and efficiently collected?" It is preferable to have the students be responsible for collecting and checking this evidence. If this is the students' responsibility, it is more likely that they will take credit for what was done or not done. Often a work log or a check-off sheet will serve as an efficient vehicle for student record keeping.

Step 3. Review the Data

Select a process for reflecting on the evidence. These brief reflections should occur at various times during the project. Possibilities might include holding a brief (1–2 minute) student-teacher conference, conducting a class discussion, or having each student fill out an index card with responses to these two questions:

1. What exactly did I accomplish?
2. What was it I did that led to this accomplishment?

Note: This could be done daily, weekly, or at any interval you deem appropriate.

Step 4. Encourage Student Reflection

Create a reflection sheet for the students to use to summarize their perceptions of the finished project or the completed test. The student submits the summary reflection with the project or immediately upon receipt of a corrected test. The focus of the reflection should be

■ Students' overall assessment of the final product, and

■ What the students learned from this experience about themselves as knowledge workers.

Behavior Management as a Potency Builder

Understandably, teachers resent the time required for effective discipline and behavior management. I believe that this is because we know that time is a zero sum commodity; we realize that if we spend time on behavior, it will reduce the time available for teaching our classes. Furthermore, to the extent that we view our jobs as teaching subject matter, we have good reason to resent this intrusion. The way I resolved this issue was doing as a friend once suggested—by making a virtue out of a necessity.

I decided I would regard myself not only as a teacher of language, reading, or social studies, but also as a teacher of personal responsibility. I could then view the time I invested in behavior management as time I spent on the personal responsibility curriculum.

The Personal Responsibility Curriculum

The two primary objectives of a personal responsibility curriculum are

1. Improving students' personal and social behavior, and

2. Helping students develop a social perspective that will lead to responsible behavior in the future.

Often teachers focus only on the first objective—changing current behavior. We determine success on the basis of immediate changes or improvement in behavior. Certainly, a desire for immediate change in behavior makes sense; if for no other reason, it is essential to preserve teacher sanity. However, we will likely set ourselves up for frustration if that is our only measure of success.

Organizational theorists frequently refer to the Pareto Principle or the 80-20 Rule (Koch, 1998). Among other things, the Pareto Principle holds that 20 percent of the participants cause 80 percent of the problems. This principle has led many managers to conclude that the best solution to a problem is to fire the 20 percent of the workers who account for 80 percent of the accidents or to expel the 20 percent of the student body responsible for 80 percent of the misbehavior. Unfortunately, experience has shown that when managers eliminate the 20 percent, another 20 percent miraculously surfaces to create 80 percent of the same problems.

I don't know what explains the 80-20 Rule or whether it is inevitable in social situations, but I do know that we teachers fool ourselves if we truly believe there exists one discipline, attendance, or behavior management system that will effectively control the behavior of every student.

However, when we focus on the second objective—helping students develop a social perspective that leads to habits of responsible behavior in the future—we are able to observe and monitor the value we are adding to our students' lives. The essence of the second part of the personal responsibility curriculum is helping students learn that their choices of behavior influence the consequences they experience.

Every approach to student management comes with a hidden curriculum. Sometimes this hidden curriculum teaches that behavior should be controlled externally. Such approaches teach that people behave because they fear being caught and punished by the teacher, the police, or the IRS. The way this message is reinforced is by emphasizing hierarchical power. The student learns that the people with the power can enforce their wishes through the delivery of punishment to the offender.

Other approaches to student management teach that behavior is controlled internally—that what influences behavior are decisions made by individuals as they weigh their personal values and the natural or logical consequences that will result from those decisions.

If our goal is to have students internalize the view that they are in control of their behavior and the consequences that flow from that behavior, then we teachers should select our classroom management strategies based on which of these two hidden curricula we wish to teach. Implementation Strategy 5.2 will help you do this.

Implementation Strategy 5.2

Monitoring and Adjusting Classroom Management Strategies

Step 1. Reflect on Your Expectations

Consider your classroom and your expectations. What positive things naturally occur, or would you like to see occur, for students who elect to engage in productive pro-social behavior? Your list might include items such as

- Esteem of classmates (natural occurrence),
- Leadership opportunities (logical occurrence),
- Good grades (natural occurrence), and
- Teacher appreciation (a natural occurrence).

Now consider the same issue in reverse. What negative things might or could occur for students who elect to engage in dysfunctional behavior? Your list might include such items as

- Rejection by classmates (natural occurrence),
- Office referrals (logical occurrence),
- Poor grades (natural occurrence), and
- Detention (logical occurrence).

Step 2. Share Your Expectations with Students

Decide how you can clearly explain to your students what constitutes the prosocial behavior that leads to positive occurrences and what constitutes the behavior that leads to the negative consequences.

Step 3. Check for Understanding

Determine the effectiveness of your explanations (Step 2) by giving the students a test on their understanding of the behavioral choices they face. Your work on this step isn't complete until every student fully understands the difference between productive and nonproductive behavior. The same principle applies to both behavior and academics—if students are expected to hit the target, they first need to see the target.

Step 4. Decide How the Management System Operates

Decide how or why students experience the consequences of their behavior. It is critical that the process you use makes it perfectly clear that it is the student's decision to engage in the behavior that triggers the consequences— not your mood, your feelings about the student, or your personal judgments.

Step 5. Make the Connection with Social Responsibility

Explain to students the two categories of consequences. Make it clear that, when the circumstances call for it, you automatically administer community consequences to make the classroom a safe and effective place for everyone. Natural consequences flow directly from a student's behavior because of the effect of those actions on other people or the environment.

Step 6. Confer with the Student

After a student experiences a consequence and the atmosphere is no longer charged with emotion, create a mechanism for the students to explain what they experienced and why. If students are able to make a connection between their choice of behavior and the consequence they experienced, you should feel good. Although the behavior the student exhibited might not have been what you wanted, the student has learned an important lesson. What should make you feel good is the success of your personal responsibility curriculum. Thanks to you, the students have developed a perspective that will serve them well for the remainder of their lives.

Teaching as a Real-World Obstacle Course

At the start of this chapter, I recited the comments we frequently hear colleagues utter when they confront all the external obstacles in the way of effective teaching and learning. These obstacles are very real. Students who have previously endured inferior schooling, who live in poverty, who battle chemical dependency, or who live with chemically dependent parents bring real issues into our classrooms. Meeting state, provincial, district, and federal mandates can make significant demands on our time and occasionally involve our students in activities that we believe are not in their best interests. To deny any of this is to put our collective heads in the sand.

However, the fact that an obstacle lies in our path does not mean it cannot be overcome. I find it instructive to look at this through the metaphor of the obstacle course. When competitors are attempting to negotiate an obstacle course, we expect that they will overcome the obstacles. The only question is, "How creatively, effectively, and speedily will the competitors do so?" When competitors complete an obstacle course and post their personal bests (see Chapter 2), those competitors don't bemoan the fact that the obstacles existed. Instead, they take pride in their ability to overcome the hurdles that were placed before them.

Please understand, I am not being so pollyannaish as to say that teachers should be thankful that circumstances beyond their control make their jobs so difficult. Furthermore, I strongly believe that educators have an obligation to organize and work politically to bring about those changes in social policy that will make universal student success and healthy child development more likely. However, while we are working on social change, we continue to be required to play the hand we are dealt.

Standards and the Need for Breakthroughs

Teachers are not the only people who confront obstacles on a daily basis. In fact, most scientists and engineers find the very presence of obstacles to be the most exciting aspect of their work. Consider the fact that scientists and engineers are engaged continuously in trying to understand things and develop solutions to things that have been deemed impossible throughout the history of humankind. After all, a scientist cannot discover something that is already known, nor can an engineer patent an idea that is already in use. In reality, the daily work of people in these fields is like the fictional Star Trekkers going "where no one has gone before."

Figuring out what has eluded everyone who has gone before is challenging. But the very headiness of it is precisely what causes people to seek out work in fields where the focus is on making breakthroughs. The role of scientists and engineers in the act of discovery explains why society so esteems their work.

It is unfortunate that teachers don't enjoy the same esteem and status, since the task before them is no less complex or heady. Just as no one has yet figured out how to cure cancer or travel to Jupiter, no one has yet identified the secret of how to educate all students to high levels of proficiency on meaningful standards—the stated goal in nearly every state and province in North America. It isn't an exaggeration to say that teachers are being asked to figure out how to "go where no one has ever gone before."

Breakthrough Technology

The process used by scientists and the business community when a challenge calls for developing new knowledge to accomplish something, heretofore deemed impossible, is called breakthrough technology. The process follows five sequential steps:

1. Envision the final product.

2. Identify all the obstacles standing in the way of realizing that vision.

3. Analyze the obstacles and affirm that these are areas where breakthroughs are needed.

4. Organize professional teams to conduct experiments and develop the needed breakthroughs.

5. Apply the knowledge (the breakthroughs) uncovered by the research teams in the production or delivery of the final product.

The five steps of Implementation Strategy 5.3 will help you to apply breakthrough technology when teaching in a standards environment.

Implementation Strategy 5.3

Applying Breakthrough Technology to Teaching in a Standards Environment

Step 1. Envision the Final Product

Where the state or province has already established high standards, the implied vision is that "Every student (regardless of the circumstances) achieves the mandated standards at high levels of proficiency."

If the state or province has not established high standards, then the visioning step will require the faculty to define for itself what excellent performance should look like and to develop a mechanism for measuring performance.

Step 2. Identify All Obstacles to Realizing the Vision

We teachers can accomplish this by asking ourselves the question, "Why is it that all our students are not currently performing as we envisioned in Step 1?" The answers we give in response to that question are our perceived obstacles.

Step 3. Analyze the Obstacles and Affirm Areas Where Breakthroughs Are Needed

At this stage, we need to examine the collective wisdom of our faculty and review the knowledge base of the profession. We need to ask, "Do any of us know the solution or does anyone know of educators elsewhere who have achieved a breakthrough that will overcome any of the obstacles we identified?" If in answering that question information surfaces on breakthroughs that have succeeded in similar school contexts, we should begin piloting those ideas. Only by trying these strategies can we see if they will succeed in the context of our school and with our students.

Step 4. Organize Professional Teams to Experiment and Develop Breakthroughs

For each of the obstacles for which no promising breakthrough has been identified, we ask teachers to volunteer to work in teams on creating the needed breakthroughs. For this strategy to work two conditions are essential: (1) the school's overall vision of universal student success on standards must be understood and supported by the entire faculty (otherwise it can not be called their shared vision); (2) all faculty members need to understand the complete master plan—the strategy of working on the breakthroughs needed to overcome the obstacles.

The reason those two conditions are so important is that once all the stakeholders understand the mission and process, then individual teachers can invest their energy in those specific areas where they have interest and expertise. Not everyone will need to participate in the development of every breakthrough.

Note: The process that teams use to make their breakthroughs is action research, which is discussed later in this chapter.

Step 5. Apply the Breakthroughs to the Production of the Final Product

As each team develops strategies to overcome the obstacles, they must share those strategies with the entire faculty. If the strategies appear viable, then field-testing should take place. If the field test produces success with your students, then teachers and administrators can spread the success throughout the school.

When we organize our work with these steps as a guide, a transformation occurs. Rather than feeling oppressed by the existence of obstacles, we can take pride in our collective, creative, and successful run through the obstacle course.

A Schoolwide Research and Development Program

Research and development (R&D) is an integral part of nearly every high-expectations endeavor in modern society. R&D focuses on a particular type of research commonly called applied research. It is important to distinguish applied research from basic scientific research. Basic research focuses on understanding the fundamentals of a science—for example, locating and understanding the properties of subatomic particles, the life cycle of a virus, or a new mathematical construct. Applied research, on the other hand, focuses on isolating the best practical applications of basic research to real-world situations.

In the case of education, research scientists in the fields of cognitive, biological, and social psychology conduct the basic research that undergirds our field. From their work, educators have learned and continue to learn basic principles about how the human brain works, and how people process, catalog, and ultimately use information. In addition, this basic research helps us understand the social behavior of humans in groups and how humans go about getting their needs met. This is important work and, like most of you, I am glad that so many bright people have dedicated their lives to these pursuits. However, it is not the work I wanted to engage in, and certainly not when I had classroom responsibilities. When teaching full-time, I had neither the interest nor the energy to spend on basic scientific research.

Applied science, however, is what I've been doing from my very first day of student teaching. This has continued to be the case with every single lesson I have taught since then. I am not alone in this. Every teacher does the same. To explain why I can assert this with total confidence, let's look at classroom teaching and see how it corresponds to the scientific method.

Teaching as Applied Research

Classroom teaching corresponds to the scientific method in the following ways:

1. I begin planning each lesson by developing and articulating an empirically verifiable research hypothesis. Generally, I won't call it that, but when I answer the question, "What do I think is the best way to help my students learn this material?" I do exactly this—I produce an empirically verifiable research hypothesis.

2. I design an experiment. The purpose of this experiment is to validate my empirically verifiable research hypothesis. Again, most of us don't find it politically correct to call our lesson plans experiments. But that is what they are. Lesson planning is where

we take what we know about learning from basic psychological research and, using our best professional judgment, design an experiment to determine the efficacy of those findings in a real-life laboratory (our classrooms).

3. No sooner do I start teaching than I begin the collecting of data and assembling a set of findings. What I observe in the students' faces while I'm at the overhead; what I see them writing on their worksheets; and what I read in their papers, projects, and tests are all data on how well my experiment is working.

4. After each lesson, I draw conclusions from my study. I usually do this in a multiple-choice format: (a) Next time I teach this material to a group of students I will do it exactly the same way; (b) Next time I teach this material to a similar group, I will change my approach as follows . . . ; or (c) Next time I will do everything in my power to avoid teaching this material.

These parallels demonstrate why I can confidently say that every day and every lesson is applied scientific research. You no doubt see teaching in the same way. But alas, one part of the scientific method is usually left out. I rarely, if ever, share my findings and conclusions from my studies with colleagues. Teaching is one of very few professions where this is the case, and we pay a heavy price. Whenever people in the R&D department of a company discover something that works or even something that doesn't, they share what they've learned so that others who are grappling with the same problem can learn from their experience.

Although sharing discoveries is important in the fields of science and engineering, it is even more critical in education. Teaching is, in reality, more complex than basic science. Teaching is a marvelously intricate mix of both art and science. Everyone knows that no two students are alike, no two teachers have identical personalities, and no two schools have identical climates and cultures. Therefore, the educational practitioner must continually experiment with novel ways to modify the general principles of teaching and learning to fit the unique circumstances of a particular classroom. Although my classes may not be identical to those of the teacher next door, there is little doubt that we still have a great deal to learn from each other about what works with the types of students who attend our school. When one considers that each school year the teacher next door conducts literally hundreds of applied research studies while you do the same, yet no viable mechanism exists for sharing what has been learned, it becomes obvious why we educators waste so much time reinventing the wheel.

Using Action Research as R&D

The type of applied research conducted by teachers is most often called action research. I have defined action research (Sagor, 2000) as "Research done by and for the person taking the action on his or her own actions, so to inform their future actions."

Earlier I introduced the five steps for using breakthrough technology to achieve our shared vision of universal student success with high standards. You recall that the focus of Step 4 was to organize teams to experiment and develop needed breakthroughs. Implementation Strategy 5.4 will help you complete that step.

Implementation Strategy 5.4

Using Teams to Develop Needed Breakthroughs

Step 1. Clarify the Shared Vision

Engage in a faculty discussion on precisely what constitutes the school's collective vision for student performance. Faculties need to take whatever time is needed for this step in order to make sure they have clarity about what is being attempted and why. Most important, it will unambiguously define what constitutes success (although this may have been done in Implementation Strategy 5.3, Step 1).

Step 2. Look for the Obstacles

Ask the question, "Why do we think (some) students are not realizing this vision now?" Review the responses to the question. What problems surfaced? Identify the breakthroughs that need to be made. Don't rush through this step, as it is important for the faculty to develop a shared understanding of exactly what obstacles lie in the way. (This step may have been done in Implementation Strategy 5.3, Step 2.)

Step 3. Create Research Teams

Invite volunteers to work collaboratively on the breakthroughs of personal interest and concern. Because there is much work to be done, it isn't productive for everyone to work on the same breakthrough (unless, of course, they want to). The entire school will ultimately learn from each team's experience. (This step may have been done in Implementation Strategy 5.3, Step 3.)

Note: It is important to consider what support or incentives might be needed for the action research study groups to be successful (e.g., release time, clerical support, graduate credit, or opportunities to use the project in their evaluation). It is important to do whatever is necessary to make sure that teachers perceive R&D as something that will meaningfully contribute to future school success. If it is viewed as a chore or an add-on that detracts from one's work, it will be resisted, resented, and ultimately abandoned.

Step 4. Make a Plan for Sharing

Schedule a time when each team can share what it has learned. After each team completes a study or inquiry, have one team member prepare a short one- to three-page summary of the team's work that can be kept in a binder for all faculty members.

As the binder expands to include the growing content of the school's R&D work, its size alone provides evidence of the collective growth of the faculty through R&D.

Figures 5.1 and 5.2 are examples of one year's R&D agendas at two schools. It may seem an unreasonable expectation that busy educators do R&D. They will find it difficult to find the time. But R&D might well be a necessity. Probably no one in your state's department of education, where the standards originated,

Figure 5.1
Research Projects at Cedar Park Elementary School

- We Think It's a Great Idea, but What Do They Think?
  Student view of a multi-age education with a thematic curriculum

- Active Learning: What It Is, What It Does
  Strategies to increase active involvement

- Choices in Learning: A Full-Day Kindergarten Perspective
  Investigation of self-directed learning

- Caught You Being a Friend
  Strategy for improving peer relationships

- Sustained Silent Reading
  Two-year look at the effects on self-esteem and interest in reading

- Issues Concerning Teaching About Safety in a Primary Classroom
  Investigation of a pilot program

- Classroom as Family: Two-Year Looping
  Effects of keeping students and teachers together

- Group Investigation in the Kindergarten Classroom
  Experience of speech- and language-delayed students

- Going Beyond the Traditional: Exploring a Continuous Progress Curriculum
  Look at multi-age classrooms

Figure 5.2
Research Projects at Franklin Roosevelt High School

- Using Students as Action Researchers
  Involving students in an exploration of our school's curriculum

- Building Dreams—Goal-Based Learning
  A strategy to develop student potential

- Where the Action Is? With the Students!
  An 11th grade English project on strategic planning

- Improving the Quality of Student Writing Through Peer and Self-Evaluation
  Motivating the reluctant writer

- Yes, You Can Do It! Nurturing Student Engagement and Persistence in Learning
  Improving math skills by building on student strengths

- The Principles of Total Quality in the Classroom
  A systems approach to teaching biology

- Relationship of Learning Styles to Student Engagement
  Using the Gregorc model in U. S. history

has figured out the secret of getting all your students to proficiency. If some people have, you should immediately invite them to come to your school and demonstrate their magic! I doubt such persons exist. So, if there is something of value that we want to achieve and no one else knows how to accomplish it (particularly with the types of students who attend our school), then who else can do this work but us!

It is unrealistic to expect to make every needed breakthrough in one year's time or even over several years. Additionally, when we do make a substantial breakthrough, it is unlikely that it will turn out to be the magic elixir that works for every teacher and every student in every situation. As teachers we realize that it will need further experimentation, modification, and revision as we move ever closer to a 100 percent success rate.

But, when teachers publicly follow the steps of breakthrough technology, when we regularly take stock of the advances we make through our action research and our focused schoolwide R&D, we will find ourselves in possession of irrefutable evidence of the continuous improvements we are making. Not only will we have evidence of our successes, which should reinforce our feelings of competence, but we will also know precisely who should be thanked for discovering the secrets to our success—ourselves. If instead, we choose to sit back and expect others to tell us how to solve our instructional problems, issues that they may neither understand nor work with on a regular basis, we are implementing a recipe for continued professional impotence.

Alternatively, when we take it upon ourselves to develop the solutions to what once appeared to be insoluble problems, we will have allowed ourselves to bathe in large, well-deserved doses of professional potency.*

---

*Research conducted as part of the "Third International Math and Science Study" (TIMSS) assessment revealed that in Japan and Germany, two countries where student performances and teacher satisfaction are often higher than in the United States, teacher collaboration on instructional problem-solving is a regular part of the school routine. It is also worth noting that in both countries teachers are provided significantly more work time devoted to this type of collaboration.

Chapter 6

Institutionalizing Optimism

Experiencing feelings of competence, belonging, usefulness, and potency are essential for self-esteem. Yet, when teachers talk of teacher and student motivation we shouldn't forget to ask the question: "Motivation for what?"

As I close this book on motivation, I think we should spend a few minutes discussing a big, transcendent, and spiritual question. What is it that makes human beings different from all God's other creatures? Why are we here? What drives us? What really matters?

Anthropologists, biologists, and philosophers have debated what makes humans unique among creatures. Some anthropologists have argued that we are the "tool makers" (Oakley, 1961). Others have pointed to the human capacity for language or our ability to reason (Tattersall, 1998; Wilson, 1978). Yet, for me what stands out as so remarkable and wondrous is the innate human capacity to dream.

To visualize that which doesn't exist, yet to believe with confidence that it can be realized, is truly something miraculous. Humans are social animals, blessed with the gift of language, therefore our personal dreams can be shared and become the collective aspirations of a community. Some dreams are large and all-encompassing, such as creating a world of harmony, peace, and prosperity. Other dreams can be important, but smaller and more focused, like building a happy, healthy, and productive family. All dreams, large or small, have in common the imagination of something different and better than what exists. Children dream of becoming adults; adults dream of building families, of creating vibrant communities, and creating a more peaceful world. Belief in our dreams is what sustains us.

To illustrate the power of dreams, consider that in 1969 a once-hapless baseball team, the New York Mets, marched to a World Series championship. The city was plastered with banners proclaiming what had become the team's motto—"We Believe!" It was inspiring to see, even for something as inconsequential as a sporting event, a city of more than nine million people transformed into a community of believers.

A Modern Necessity

The power and the need to believe that we will ultimately succeed in realizing our dreams has never been more important. In these days when instant communication links the farthest corners of the world, we share in each other's fears and tragedies, as well as our successes. Television brings terrorism, war, and famine into our living rooms. The shrinking world combined with around the clock news puts us at risk of feeling overwhelmed. Having something to believe in, to strive for, and to dream about is essential if we are to have the energy to prevail. This need brings us to the last and most essential aspect of CBUPO—optimism.

The Importance of Optimism for Youth

From their earliest days, children know that they will grow up to be adults. But what characterizes the life they will live? Instinctively, to get answers to this question, young people look to the adults in their lives for clues. Most children assume, quite logically, that what life holds for them is identical to or similar to what life has provided for the significant adults in their lives. For example, if young people see around them happy, self-actualized adults, individuals who are contributing to the well-being of their families and their communities, enjoying good health, and excitedly looking forward to the future, they will assume that the same will hold true for them.

Unfortunately, the reverse is also true. When children regularly observe adults who are struggling with poverty, racism, depression, alienation, and substance abuse, they logically suspect that this is what is in store for them.

Although educators can understand the optimism of children surrounded by positive influences, we can as easily comprehend the causes for the pessimism that seems to control the outlook of the less fortunate children. However, we need not despair for the latter child. We have ample evidence that optimism can be generated in even the darkest of circumstances. Resiliency can, in fact, be developed and nurtured.

Many readers may remember the celebrated case of philanthropist Eugene Lang, who several years ago promised a class of New York 6th graders, who were in a school with an eventual dropout rate that approached 90 percent, a fully paid college education. All he asked the students to do was work hard and stay out of trouble. Although none of the students had reasons for optimism until that day, all but one student accepted the challenge, graduated from high school, and went on to college (Levin, 2001). Since that time, several other cases have demonstrated that a sincere promise, coupled with a helping hand, can bring hope where before there had been only despair.

Jaime Escalante, made famous in the movie *Stand and Deliver,* assured hundreds of poor Latino students at Garfield High School, a barrio high school in East Los Angeles, that in spite of their weak math skills they could outperform the best and brightest students in the United States on the rigorous advanced placement exam in calculus. Several hundred students took his challenge and their collective performance was superior to nearly every other high school in the country (Mathews, 1988).

Nourishing Optimism

In our classrooms, teachers see both types of students—those who have high hopes and inspiring dreams, and those who are equally sure they will see no gold pot at the end of the rainbow. The most important part of our job is nourishing the optimism of the dreamers while planting and nurturing the seeds of optimism in those students where none now exists.

Teachers need to provide students with the three elements that were demonstrated in the experience of the children helped by Eugene Lang and Jaime Escalante:

1. A compelling vision,
2. A viable support system, and
3. Continuous credible evidence of progress.

In the cases of Lang and Escalante, the compelling vision was being able to feast on the world of opportunity available to those with a college degree. The support system included high-quality teaching, caring, and ongoing guidance from Lang and Escalante themselves. Finally, the mentors paved the road with checkpoints, or mileposts, by which the students could see continuous and credible evidence of their progress.

Teachers don't need to have the financial wherewithal of Lang or the energy and charisma of Escalante. The CBUPO building processes discussed in this book, or other strategies of your own invention, can just as easily provide these critical elements for your students.

The Importance of Optimism for Adults

In the previous chapter, I discussed the concept of breakthrough technology. I pointed out that the endeavor of going where no one has gone before powerfully motivates adults. But, just as with youth, the motivation necessary for the pursuit of a once impossible dream requires the presence of five critical elements:

1. A compelling vision,
2. Support,
3. Opportunities for creativity,
4. Opportunities for collaboration, and
5. A productive professional culture.

For optimism to reign at school, the atmosphere and environment where we work must nourish the belief that things can and will improve. This begins with focusing on these five essential elements and finding ways to institutionalize them in the professional culture of our schools.

Compelling Vision

Wherever breakthrough technology has succeeded, things began with a compelling vision. NASA envisioned the landing of a man on the moon, Jonas Salk foresaw an end to polio, and computer scientists working in a garage imagined placing a personal computer on every worker's desk. None of these very real accomplishments would or could have occurred without a compelling vision.

In our roles as individual teachers, members of school faculties, and practitioners of education, we need to envision what universal student success could look like, what it would mean, and how wonderful it would be to achieve. We need to articulate this vision for ourselves, for each other, and for the communities we serve. Just as we depend on the confidence and optimism of our doctors that medicine will one day find cures for the diseases that might befall us in the future, our communities need to see our confidence and optimism that we will succeed at making the necessary breakthroughs for universal student success.

Support

Without the political and financial support as well as the enthusiastic cheerleading of the U. S. public, the moon landing would never have occurred. Likewise, without the sponsorship of his research and the support of the larger medical community, Salk wouldn't have produced his vaccine.

For educators, this support is, unfortunately, one of those obstacles we will need to confront and overcome—often with methods and devices of our own invention. In these times of public monetary belt tightening, tangible support for our work is hard to come by. However, human support is abundant.

Belief in the importance of educational excellence has never been higher. Recent polls indicate the willingness of U.S. citizens to pay for school improvement (Rose & Gallup, 2000, 2001). More critical, the belief in the importance of education remains incredibly high among the parents of the poorest and most disadvantaged students (Rose & Gallup, 2001). Educators need to take advantage of the public's hunger for improvement. But to do so, we need to increase our effectiveness in galvanizing all the good will and support that exists. Sharing our optimism, our data, and our enthusiasm is one good way to start.

Opportunities for Creativity

When attempting to go where everyone wants to go but where no one has gone before, new routes need to be discovered or created. If our predecessors knew how to accomplish universal success, they would have done so. Since they didn't, we know it will take creative invention to succeed. One of the opportunities provided by the standards movement is that the focus is now on the ends of education, as opposed to the means. Clearly, it is folly to expect new and different results from old methods. No one expects an engineer or scientist to commit energy toward the achievement of a novel outcome while following a tired old recipe. However, it doesn't take much coaxing to encourage a professional to collaboratively create, innovate, and experiment to make significant breakthroughs.

The public needs to view educators as welcoming the challenge of standards and the goal of universal student success. Policymakers, as well as the community, will warmly receive our supportive posture. Yet, we must make it perfectly clear that our commitment is conditional. We agree to hold ourselves accountable for continuous progress toward the attainment of a compelling vision (universal student success), but, in exchange, we must be empowered and trusted to creatively design the instructional innovations required to make that happen.

Opportunities for Collaboration

Frequently, educators speak of collaboration as though working collaboratively is somehow inherently superior to working alone. Sure, most educators are people persons and, consequently, often find group work more enjoyable than working in isolation. But this inclination toward group work doesn't make collaboration necessarily any better than other types of work. However, when an individual attempts to solve a problem that has proven difficult to others, the task is unlikely to inspire the optimism necessary for success. It is for this reason that in the high-tech industries, in the fields of science and engineering, and, increasingly, in the competitive business world, professionals are organized into teams to solve perplexing problems.

Productive Professional Cultures

If we teachers truly want to foster optimism in these times of high expectations, high-stakes testing, and the challenge of universal student success, we need to attend to the professional culture of the school. Increasingly, research has shown that the professional culture of an organization is the single best predictor of success (Rosenholtz, 1991; Little, 1982; Shein, 1992). Specifically, researchers in schools and businesses have concluded that to prevail with formidable challenges, the workplace needs to manifest the cultural attributes of a professional learning community (Senge, 1990, 1999; DuFour & Eaker, 1998).

Based on a review of the research on professional learning communities and building on the work of Saphier and King (1985), I compiled a list of 14 norms that had been shown to be correlates of school effectiveness. Using these norms, I developed a self-report survey (Figure 6.1) to be used by school faculties to determine the perceived presence or absence of these norms in their school's culture.

My research (Sagor, 1992a, 1992b) revealed that in schools where the culture was rated as high on these 14 norms, optimism prevailed, and faculty morale was high. In those schools, student performance continuously improved.

From these data, we concluded that in environments that support CBUPOs for teachers, the students prosper. Implementation Strategy 6.1 explains how to use the culture survey to take stock of your school's professional culture.

Figure 6.1
School Culture Survey

Schools differ in many ways. One difference is the character of their organizational culture. The culture of an organization can be seen through the shared norms, values, and behavior of members of the community. This survey asks you to think about your school as a workplace, and to assess the degree to which you see each of the following norms or values as consistent features of the work life of the school. It is important that you score the school on each norm.

Please rate your school (as a whole) on each of these norms or values using the following scale:

1 = Almost always characteristic of our school
2 = Generally characteristic of our school
3 = Seldom characteristic of our school
4 = Not characteristic of our school

Norm or Value	Rating	Recent Illustrative Example*
1. **Collegiality** Professional collaboration on educational issues		
2. **Experimentation** Interest in exploring new, not yet proven techniques		
3. **High Expectations** A pervasive push for high performance for students and teachers		
4. **Trust and Confidence** A pervasive feeling that people will do what's right		
5. **Tangible Support** Financial and material assistance that supports teaching and learning		
6. **Reaching Out to the Knowledge Base** Use of research, reading of professional journals, and attending workshops		

continued

Figure 6.1
School Culture Survey—*Continued*

Norm or Value	Rating	Recent Illustrative Example*
7. **Appreciation and Recognition** Acknowledgment of high-quality student and faculty work and effort		
8. **Caring–Celebration–Humor**		
9. **Appreciation of Leadership** Leadership provided by teachers, principals, and other professional staff		
10. **Clarity of Goals**		
11. **Protection of What's Important** School goals and priorities		
12. **Involvement of Stakeholders in Decision Making** Those who will be affected by decisions are involved in making them		
13. **Traditions** Rituals and events that celebrate and support core school values		
14. **Honest, Open Communication**		

*For each norm or value that you rate as 1 or 2, please provide a recent example of how that norm was demonstrated through individual or organizational behavior.

Implementation Strategy 6.1

Taking Stock of Your School's Culture

Step 1. Collect the Data

Have your faculty complete the school culture survey in Figure 6.1. Schedule this activity at a faculty meeting so that you achieve nearly a 100-percent response rate. When doing this in a large secondary school, have the respondents rate the culture of their departments as well, since departmental work groups have a culture unto themselves (McLaughlin & Talbert, 2001).

Step 2. Collect More Data

Place 14 posters around the room, one for each norm (see Figure 6.2). Provide each teacher with 14 sticky dots.

Figure 6.2
School Culture Norm 3, High Expectations

Post a piece of chart paper divided into quadrants for each of the 14 norms in the School Culture Survey. Give participants 14 sticky dots to place in the quadrant that corresponds with their answer to each question. Use these posters as a handy visual in tracking your school's score on the School Culture Survey.

1 (Always Characteristic)	3 (Seldom Characteristic)
2 (Generally Characteristic)	4 (Not Characteristic)
_____ (1s and 2s) = _____ %	_____ (3s and 4s) = _____ %

After everyone has completed the survey, provide a break and ask teachers to place their dots in the quadrant that corresponds to their rating.

Step 3. Compute the Norms

Compile the results by totaling the dots on the left-hand side of each poster (the scores of one and two) and the dots on the right-hand side (the scores of three and four). Whenever the ones and twos total 75 percent or more of the total, you may conclude that this norm exists in your school or department (see Figure 6.3). Where the ones and twos total less than 75 percent (see Figure 6.4), it means that those behaviors may be present in the work environment, but they aren't prevalent enough to constitute a cultural norm.

Step 4. Look at the Strength and Distribution of Scores

Examine the strength of the norms. Take a look at the distribution of the dots. Are they clustered together (as in Figure 6.3)? If so, not only can you say this is a norm, but you can also say it is a tightly held norm. If the participants scattered the dots throughout the four quadrants (as in

Figure 6.3
School Culture Norm 1, Collegiality

Example of results from posting the school culture survey

1 (Always Characteristic)	3 (Seldom Characteristic)
2 (Generally Characteristic)	4 (Not Characteristic)

__19__ (1s and 2s) = __82.6__ %   __4__ (3s and 4s) = __17.4__ %

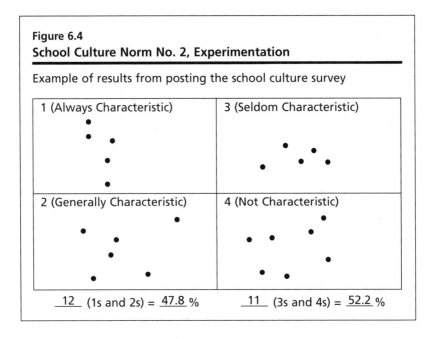

Figure 6.4
School Culture Norm No. 2, Experimentation

Figure 6.4), it indicates that the members of your school or department community are experiencing this factor quite differently.

Step 5. Examine the Implications

Discuss the implications of the data. To the degree that you are pleased to see a strong and productive norm (Figure 6.3), you should acknowledge that fact and make a point of nurturing those behaviors so they will stay strong. Where you note a weak or absent norm (Figure 6.4), discuss how it might be strengthened to make working in the school or department a more satisfying and successful experience for all.

A Community of Optimism

I'm sure every historical period has had its defining moments. Today, because of technological advances, everyone can share those moments as a world community in a way we never could before. Two such moments loom large in my memory.

Less than 10 years after President John Kennedy challenged the people of the United States to "land a man on the moon and return him safely to earth before the end of the decade," Neil Armstrong stepped onto the surface of the moon proclaiming, "This is one small step for man, one giant leap for mankind." An entire nation, and an entire world, took pride in this collective accomplishment of humankind. We all dreamed it; we worked at it; we made the breakthroughs; and then we realized the dream.

Another moment I frequently reflect on also deals with a dream. This one, unfortunately, is not yet realized. After having great success stirring the conscience of the people of the United States, Martin Luther King Jr. stood on the steps of the Lincoln Memorial to address the multitude gathered for the great 1964 March on Washington. King began that speech with the immortal words, "I have a dream. . . ."

He did not live to see his dream realized. But dreams need not be fully realized to continue to inspire optimism and action. We have yet to realize the dream of true equality of opportunity for all children in the United States. But the dream lives on. King's vision, his writings, and that famous speech continue to inspire and produce optimism whenever anyone reads or hears them.

Recently it has been asserted that closing the achievement gap and creating universal school success is the great civil rights struggle of the 21st century. The success of that struggle and realization of that dream rests on the optimism we transmit to our colleagues, our students, and our communities.

Stimulating student motivation and nurturing excellence in teaching require that we work and learn in cultures of optimism. If we commit ourselves to ensuring that every day, every teacher and every student experiences authentic feelings of competence, belonging, usefulness, and potency, we are well on our way to realizing that dream.

References
and Resources

Boyer, E. L. (1983). *High school: A report on secondary education in America.* New York: Harper & Row.

Campbell, L., Campbell, B., & Dickinson, D. (2003). *Teaching and learning through multiple intelligences* (3rd ed.). Boston: Allyn and Bacon.

Cloer, T. & Alexander, W. A., Jr. (1992). Inviting teacher characteristics and teacher effectiveness: A preliminary study. *Journal of Invitational Theory and Practice, 1*(1), 31–42.

Delisle, R. (1997). *How to use problem-based learning in the classroom.* Alexandria, VA: Association for Supervision and Curriculum Development.

DuFour, R., & Eaker, R. E. (1998). *Professional learning communities at work: Best practices for enhancing student achievement.* Alexandria, VA: Association for Supervision and Curriculum Development; and Bloomington, IN: National Educational Service.

Education of All Handicapped Children Act, Volume Source § 94-142 (1975).

Fullan, M. (1993). *Change forces: Probing the depth of educational reform.* New York: Falmer Press.

Gardner, H. (1999). *Intelligence reframed: Multiple intelligences for the 21st century.* New York: BasicBooks.

Gaustad, J. (1993, March). Peer and cross-age tutoring. *ERIC Digest 79.* Eugene: ERIC Clearinghouse on Educational Management, University of Oregon.

Gibson, M., & Ogbu, J. (Eds.). (1991). *Minority status and schooling: A comparative study of immigrant and involuntary minorities.* New York: Garland.

Glasser, W. (1998a). *Choice theory: A new psychology of personal freedom.* New York: HarperCollins.

Glasser, W. (1998b). *The quality school: Managing students without coercion.* New York: HarperPerennial.

Glatthorn, A. A. (1987). *Curriculum leadership.* Glenview, IL: Scott Foresman.

Glickman, C. D. (1993). *Renewing America's schools: A guide for school-based action.* San Francisco: Jossey-Bass.

Greene, J. P. (2002, April). *High school graduation rates in the United States.* (Report). New York: Center for Civic Innovation.

Koch, R. (1998). *The 80/20 principle: The secret of achieving more with less.* New York: Currency.

Kinsley, C. W., & McPherson, K. (Eds.). (1995). *Enriching the curriculum through service learning.* Alexandria, VA: Association for Supervision and Curriculum Development.

Levin, C. (2001, November 16). *In recognition of the Eugene M. Lang I Have A Dream Foundation.* 107th Cong., 1st Sess.

Little, J. W. (1982). Norms of collegiality and experimentation: Workplace conditions of school success. *American Educational Research Journal, 19*(3), 325–340.

Mathews, J. (1988). *Escalante: The best teacher in America.* New York: Holt.

McCarthy, B. (1987). *About teaching: 4MAT in the classroom.* Wauconda, IL: About Learning.

McCarthy, B. (1997, March). A tale of four learners: 4MAT's learning styles. *Educational Leadership 54*(6).

McLaughlin, M. W., & Talbert, J. E. (2001). *Professional communities and the work of high school teaching.* University of Chicago Press.

Oakley, K. P. (1961). *Man the tool-maker* (5th ed.). London: Trustees of the British Museum.

Ogbu, J. (1991). *Cultural models and educational strategies of non-dominant peoples.* New York: City College Press.

Powell, A. G., Farrar, E., & Cohen, D. K. (1985). *The shopping mall high school: Winners and losers in the educational marketplace.* Boston: Houghton Mifflin.

Purkey, W. W., & Novak, J. (1996). *Inviting school success: A self-concept approach to teaching, learning, and democratic practice* (3rd ed.). Belmont, CA: Wadsworth.

Purkey, W. W., & Strahan, D. (1995). School transformation through invitational education. *Research in the Schools, 2*(2), 1–6.

Rose, L. C., & Gallup, A. M. (2000). The 32nd annual Phi Delta Kappa/Gallup Poll of the public's attitudes toward the public schools. *Phi Delta Kappan, 82*(1), 41–57.

Rose, L. C., & Gallup, A. M. (2001). The 33nd annual Phi Delta Kappa/Gallup Poll of the public's attitudes toward the public schools. *Phi Delta Kappan, 83*(1), 41–58.

Rosenholtz, S. J. (1991). *Teacher's workplace: The social organization of schools.* New York: Teachers College Press.

Sagor, R. D. (1992a, April). *Collaborative action research: A cultural mechanism for school development and professional restructuring?* Paper presented at the annual meeting of the American Educational Research Association, San Francisco.

Sagor, R. D. (1992b, April). *An exploration of the impact of district context upon school culture: Implications for effectiveness.* Paper presented at the annual meeting of the American Educational Research Association, San Francisco. (ERIC Document Reproduction Service No. ED 024 386)

Sagor, R. (1991, April). Effective schooling: Lessons from the athletic field. *NASSP Bulletin, 75*(534), 95–101.

Sagor, R. (1996). *Local control and accountability: How to get it, keep it, and improve school performance*. Thousand Oaks, CA: Corwin.

Sagor, R. (2000). *Guiding school improvement with action research*. Alexandria, VA: Association for Supervision and Curriculum Development.

Saphier, J., & King, M. (1985). Good seeds grow in strong cultures. *Educational Leadership, 42*, 67–73.

Senge, P. (1990). *The fifth discipline: The art and practice of the learning organization*. New York: Doubleday/Currency.

Senge, P. M. (1999). *The dance of change: The challenges to sustaining momentum in learning organizations*. New York: Currency/Doubleday.

Shein, E. H. (1992). *Organizational culture and leadership*. San Francisco: Jossey-Bass.

Silver, H. F., Strong, R. W., & Perini, M. J. (2000). *So each may learn: Integrating learning styles and multiple intelligences*. Alexandria, VA: Association for Supervision and Curriculum Development.

Sizer, T. R. (1992). *Horace's compromise: The dilemma of the American high school*. Boston: Houghton-Mifflin.

Slavin, R. E. (1994). *Using student team learning* (4th ed.). Baltimore: Johns Hopkins Team Learning Project.

Stanley, P. H., & Purkey, W. W. (1994). Student self-concept-as-learner: Does invitational education make a difference? *Research in the Schools, 1*(2), 15–22.

Tattersall, I. (1998). *Becoming human: Evolution and human uniqueness*. New York: Harcourt Brace.

Torp, L., & Sage, S. (2002). *Problems as possibilities: Problem-based learning for K–16 education* (2nd ed.). Alexandria, VA: Association for Supervision and Curriculum Development.

Wehlage, G. G., Rutter, R. A., Smith, G. A., Lesko, N., and Fernandez, R. R. (1989). *Reducing the risk: Schools as communities of support*. New York: Falmer Press.

Wilson, E. O. (1978). *On human nature*. Cambridge: Harvard University Press.

Zajonc, R. B. (1984). The interaction of affect and cognition. In K. R. Scherer & P. Ekman (Eds.), *Approaches to emotion*. Hillsdale, NJ: Erlbaum.

Zajonc, R. B., & McIntosh, D. N. (1992). Emotions research: Some promising questions and some questionable promises. *Psychological Science, 3*, 70–74.

Index

Page numbers followed by an *f* indicate reference to a figure.

About the Author

Richard Sagor is the founder and director of the Institute for the Study of Inquiry in Education (ISIE), an organization that provides support and consulting services to schools, school districts, and educational organizations striving to increase equity and excellence in student performance. Before ISIE, Sagor was an associate professor of educational leadership at Washington State University for 10 years.

During his 17 years in public schools, Sagor was a teacher, principal, and assistant superintendent. For the past 15 years, he has facilitated workshops for educators throughout the United States and internationally on using data for school improvement, conducting action research, and improving student motivation and leadership development.

Sagor has frequently contributed articles to *Educational Leadership* and is the author of two other ASCD books, *How to Conduct Collaborative Action Research* and *Guiding School Improvement with Action Research*. Other books include *At Risk Students: Reaching and Teaching Them, The TQE Principal: A Transformed Leader*, and *Local Control and Accountability: How to Get it, Keep it, and Improve School Performance*.

You may reach the author at the Institute for the Study of Inquiry in Education (ISIE), 16420 SE McGillivray, Suite 103-239, Vancouver, WA 98683 USA. Phone: (360) 834-3503. E-mail: rdsagor@ isie.org.

Related ASCD Resources: Motivation

At the time of publication, the following ASCD resources were available; for the most up-to-date information about ASCD resources, go to www.ascd.org. ASCD stock numbers are noted in parentheses.

Audiotapes

Motivating Students Who Don't Care by Allen Mendler (#503221)
Motivating Students and Teachers in an Era of Standards
    by Richard Sagor (#503252)

Networks

Visit the ASCD Web site (www.ascd.org) and search for "networks" for information about professional educators who have formed groups around topics like "Quality Education," "Differentiated Instruction," and "Multiple Intelligences." Look in the "Network Directory" for current facilitators' addresses and phone numbers.

Videotapes

Mentoring the New Teacher: Motivating Students (#494011)
A Visit to a Motivated Classroom (#403384)

For more information, visit us on the World Wide Web (http://www.ascd.org), send an e-mail message to member@ascd.org, call the ASCD Service Center (1-800-933-ASCD or 703-578-9600, then press 2), send a fax to 703-575-5400, or write to Information Services, ASCD, 1703 N. Beauregard St., Alexandria, VA 22311-1714 USA.